George Hugg

Songs of the mercy seat

A new collection for Sunday-schools, Christian endeavor, Epworth league, young

people's meetings, revival, camp and prayer

George Hugg

Songs of the mercy seat
A new collection for Sunday-schools, Christian endeavor, Epworth league, young people's meetings, revival, camp and prayer

ISBN/EAN: 9783337266226

Printed in Europe, USA, Canada, Australia, Japan

Cover: Foto ©Thomas Meinert / pixelio.de

More available books at **www.hansebooks.com**

A NEW COLLECTION

—FOR—

Sunday-Schools, Christian Endeavor, Epworth League, Young People's Meetings, Revival, Camp and Prayer Meetings, Choirs and the Home Circle.

—BY—

GEORGE C. HUGG and POWELL G. FITHIAN.

Price, $25.00 per hundred; 30 cents, singly.

PUBLISHED BY

GEORGE C. HUGG,

2133 Newkirk St., Philadelphia, Pa.

...Preface...

IN presenting "SONGS OF THE MERCY-SEAT" for public favor we feel sure that much good will be derived from the correct singing of the many gems found within its cover. We urge all interested in a new book to examine it very carefully.

GEO. C. HUGG,

POWELL G. FITHIAN,

Editors.

WARNING.

SONGS OF THE MERCY SEAT.

HE SAYS SO IN HIS WORD.

Rev. Johnson Oatman, Jr.

Powell G. Fithian.

1. O list - en to this sto - 'ry, The sweetest ev - er heard;
2. He saw poor sin - ners dy - ing, With love his bo - som stirred;
3. My heart's no long - er heav - y, But light as an - y bird;
4. I'm glad I sought the Sav - iour, Al - tho' so long de - ferred;

Christ Je - sus died for sin - ners, He says so in his Word.
He died for their sal - va - tion, He says so in his Word.
Be - cause my Sav - iour loves me, He says so in his Word.
I'll live with him for - ev - er, He says so in his Word.

CHORUS.

He says so in his Word, He says so in his Word;

rit.

Christ Je - sus died for sin - ners, He says so in his Word.

HOME OF THE SOUL.

A. S. D.

A. S. DOUGHTY.

1. Soon trials and conflicts of life will be o'er, And we shall have crossed the dark main;
2. Faith's rapturous vision may sometimes behold An outline of heaven-ly scene;
3. That city of jewels, and mansions untold, And walls made of jasper sublime;
4. A land that's so pure and so free from all sin, Where pain never uttered a cry;
5. When we with the saints and the glorified throng Assemble upon that blest shore,

Earth's pleasures forsaken we'll never deplore, If heaven's blest portal we gain.
As Mo-ses beheld the fair Canaan of old, Far off, with a Jordan be - tween.
Refulgent with lustre, like transparent gold, And never corroded by time.
Where sickness and death cannot enter therein, And nothing that maketh a lie.
With harps and with voices we'll chant the new song With heaven's redeemed evermore.

CHORUS.

We're nearing the shore of that beautiful land, That far-away home of the soul ;......

And soon we will stand on that glittering strand, And chant while the ages shall roll.

AT THE DOOR.

5

Thomas MacKellar.   Geo. C. Hugg.

With feeling.

1. At the door of mercy sigh - ing With the burden of my sin,
2. I have sought to earn thy fa - vor, Car - ing not for toil or cost,
3. Hark! what sounds mine ear re - ceiv - eth, Sweet as songs of ser - a - phim!
4. I knew not of Je - sus' kind - ness! I knew not of Je - sus' grace!

Day and night my soul is cry - ing, "O - pen, Lord, and let me in."
Yet I find not him, my Sav - iour, He who came to seek the lost.
"He that in the Lord be - liev - eth Life e - ter - nal hath in him."
O the blackness of the blind - ness That could not behold his face!

Wait - ing 'mid the darkness drea - ry, Stretching out my hands to thee,
Bless - ed Master! in thy pit - y Teach me what I ought to do,
At the out - er door why stay - ing? Nothing, soul, hast thou to pay:
I saw not the door was o - pen, Nor my Lord in - vite me in:

Ral - len - tan - do.

In the ref - uge for the wea - ry Is there not a place for me?
So that in the ho - ly cit - y I may gain an entrance too.
Christ in love to thee is say - ing, Wea - ry child, come in to - day.
Grace is mine beyond my hop - ing, Mer - cy mightier than my sin.

a tempo. ff   *pp*   *rit.*

At the door I'm crying let me in! At the door I'm crying let me in!

THERE IS PARDON FOR YOU.

Mrs. Frank A. Breck.

Powell G. Fithian.

1. There's a won-der-ful Saviour of sin - ners, dear soul, And wonder-ful
2. There's a won-der-ful Saviour of sin - ners, dear soul, Com-passionate

things he will do, If you will but yield to his bless-ed con-trol And
faithful and true; With love that restoreth the sor - row-ing soul, And

take what he of-fers to you. There's a wonderful healing that maketh you
giv-eth full pardon to you. There's a won-derful Giver of gladness, dear

whole; A pow'r that will cleanse and renew; A wonder-ful Saviour of
soul, Of joy that the world never knew; And riv-ers of gladness shall

Chorus.

sin-ners, dear soul, Who of-fers full pardon to you.
o - ver you roll, If Jesus gives pardon to you.

O yes, there is

pardon for you,........ A won-der-ful pardon for you; Take the
for you,

message I give, O believe it and live ; O yes, there is pardon for you.

ARLINGTON. C. M.

Rev. I. Watts.

Thos. A. Arne.

1. Am I a sol-dier of the cross, A foll'wer of the Lamb,
2. Must I be carried to the skies On flow'ry beds of ease,
3. Are there no foes for me to face? Must I not stem the flood?
4. Since I must fight if I would reign, Increase my cour-age, Lord;

And shall I fear to own his cause, Or blush to speak his name?
While oth-ers fought to win the prize, And sailed thro' blood-y seas?
Is this vile world a friend to grace, To help me on to God?
I'll bear the toil, en-dure the pain, Sup-port-ed by thy Word.

I HAVE ABANDONED ALL.

Rev. John L. Newkirk.   Powell G. Fithian.

1. I have a-bandoned my all to my Fa-ther, To him I'm willing my
2. Years I had lived and had walked in the sun-light, Respite from guilt of my
3. Oft were the moments when self hid my Saviour, Trials would come, and then
4. Then Je-sus led me to see the way clear-ly, Just to renounce all and

all to re-sign; I can do nothing, how deep-ly I feel it,
sins I en-joyed; But there a-rose in my heart a deep long-ing
conquered I'd be; I was dis-couraged, O God, will there ev-er,
let him con-trol; Oh, how the tem-ple was flood-ed with glo-ry!

Chorus.

He gives me vic-t'ry thro' his grace di-vine.
To have the old life with-in me destroyed.
Ev-er in this life, be freedom for me? } Yes, I'm a-bandoned,
What a deep qui-et per-vad-ed my soul.

ful-ly a-bandoned un-to the Ho-ly Ghost's perfect control; Oh, hal-le-

lu-jah! he fills the tem-ple, Billows of glo-ry sweep o-ver my soul!

J. Harry Crossley.   Geo. Beaverson.   By per.

1. From Calv'ry's mount there free- ly flows The stream of sal-vation thro' Je - sus;
2. The sto - ry old I love to tell, Of Jesus who now lives in glo - ry;
3. No oth - er way to man is giv'n, To gain this salvation, but Je - sus;
4. Oh, come and prove his mighty pow'r, To save you and keep you from fall- ing;

And he its cleansing pow- er knows Who's washed in its life giv- ing flood.
My griefs and sorrows on him fell, Who died that my soul might be free.
He is the Lord of earth and heav'n, His blood will a- tone for all   sin.
He calls you now, this ver - y hour; Ac- cept his sal - va- tion and live.

Refrain.

'Tis flow - ing,   flow - ing, The stream of sal - va - tion is flow - ing;

'Tis flow - ing,   flow - ing, 'Tis flowing for you and for   me.

CONTENTMENT.

IDA L. REED.   (A PRAYER.)   POWELL G. FITHIAN.

Andante.

1. Je - sus, Sav - iour, let me be,   Whereso - e'er I am content ;
2. Hum-ble tho' my sphere may be,   All the lit - tle good I can
3. Teach me how to serve thee best,   As the days are glid - ing by ;
4. Let me dai - ly sing thy praise,   Winning oth - er souls to thee ;

Giv - ing all my life to thee,   Let my days be wise - ly spent.
I would do most cheer- ful - ly,   E'er o - bey-ing thy command.
Let thy bless- ing on me rest,   Keep me ev - er to thee nigh.
On thy ho - ly, bless-ed ways,   Je - sus, Sav- iour, lead thou me.

CHORUS.

All a - long my earthly way,   Wheresoe'er my steps may stray,

Do - ing all I can for thee,   Je - sus, Saviour, let me be.

Anna D. Bradley.   E. M. Douthit.

1. Soul, are you wea-ry of wand'ring? Soul, would you find the   light?
2. Soul, would you journey in safe-ty, Fearing no wind, no   wave?
3. Soul, would you lose all your bur-den? Would you have peace with-in?
4. Soul, do not wait an-y long-er; Come, or the call may   cease:

Je-sus is wait-ing to bless you; Heed the first call to-night.
Heed then this call of your Mas-ter; Je-sus a-lone can   save.
Heed then this call of the Sav-iour; Turn now a-way from   sin.
Now he is of-fer-ing par-don, Now he is off'ring   peace.

Chorus.

Soul, it is you that the Mas-ter Calls while he holds the   light;

Soul, if you care for a Sav-iour, Heed the first call to-night.

ALIVE IN CHRIST.

Rev. Isaac N. Wilson.   Wm. J. Kirkpatrick.

1. A - live in Christ! O hap - py day When from the death of sin I rose;
2. A - live in Christ! I grow in grace, And joyous tread the upward road;
3. 'Tis done, complete in Christ I stand; All for-mer joys are lost in this—

Sweet was the new birth's glorious thrill, And day by day 'tis sweeter still,
Hold-ing communion sweet with God, I pass the mystic vales of sin:
The deep, subdued sub - du- ing bliss, Lord, I am naught: thou, thou art all;

A - live in Christ! my spir- it glows And my glad heart sings on its way,
A - live in Christ! yes, all with-in Is purged from guilt and pu- ri- fied;
May thy sweet peace for - ev - er fall On me, for my poor will is gone,

As it recounts the wondrous word That reconciled me to the Lord.
I clos - er seek my Saviour's side, And joy to see his smiling face.
Thine is the best, let thine be done; For so I love thee, O my God.

A. S. DOUGHTY.

GEO. C. HUGG.

Spirited.

1. Life's clos-ing hours pass sweetly by, Earth's pains are felt no more;
2. With tri-als and with conflicts past, And rec-ord placed on high,
3. The part-ing veil re-veals the tide, Where on the mar-gin wait
4. As na-ture sinks in death's embrace, So will my spir-it rise

To heav'n I now di-rect mine eye To view the shining shore.
By faith I see the crown at last, And vic-t'ry drawing nigh.
My friends redeemed, the glo-ri-fied, To sweep me thro' the gate.
Tri-umphant thro' re-deeming grace, To rest in par-a-dise.

CHORUS.

Home - ward, home - ward, Home to the shin - ing shore;
Onward, upward, we are marching,

Home - ward, home - ward, Home to the shin - ing shore.
Onward, upward, we are marching,

TRUSTING ALL TO JESUS.

C. E. F.

CHAS. E. FERGUSON.

1. Brother, on life's storm-y o-cean, Be not lost in doubt and fear;
2. Tho' temp-ta- tions may surround you, And you feel your feet would fall,
3. Blessed com - fort 'tis in knowing There is rest on yon - der shore;

Look be-- yond the waves' commo- tion, Christ, the Lord, is ev - er near.
With his lov - ing arms a- round you, Trust the Sav - iour thro' it all.
While the path is brighter growing, Let us love him more and more.

CHORUS.

He is near, O call up - on him, There's no oth - er friend so true;

He is near, O call up - on him, Let him lead you safe - ly through.

I WILL FOLLOW THEE, MY JESUS.

Rev. John L. Newkirk.   Powell G. Fithian.

1. I will fol-low thee, my Je-sus, Where thou leadest, I will go;
2. It may be that thou wilt take me Thro' a dark and storm-y way;
3. Yes, I'll fol-low, glad-ly fol-low, For I've reckoned up the cost,

Will not murmur; will not question; Sim-ply fol-low, here be-low.
Loss of friends and death may test me, Je-sus, on-ly, will I say.
And with Je-sus, precious Je-sus, I will count all things, but lost.

CHORUS.

I will fol-low with my Je-sus, I will fol-low an-y-where;

I will fol-low, yes, I'll fol-low With my Je-sus an-y-where.

BETHESDA.

MARY A. MCKEE.   ADAM GEIBEL.

Slowly and with great expression.

1. I come, O Lord, when troubled waves are stirring The healing fount that
2. I come, O Lord, when mercy is extend - ed, And an - gel wings are
3. I come, O Lord, tho' oth- ers may be hast-ing With stronger steps to

cures the touch of sin; I come in hope, no faintness then de-
brooding soft - ly o'er The ways of sin, that I had once de-
seek the way of life; I come in faith, no precious moment

ter - ing, But there are none, O Lord, to help me in.
fend - ed, I leave them all, and I can do no more.
wast - ing, While earth and heav'n with love and peace are rife.

REFRAIN. QUARTET.

Help me in, help me in! I am tir - ed now of sin;
Help me in, help me in!

Inst.

Help me in,.......... help me in !........ I may life e - ter - nal win !
Oh,   help me in,   oh,   help me in !

GOD IS LOVE.

C. H. S.   1 John 4: 16.   Acts 17: 28.   CLARA H. SCOTT.

1. God is Love; that Love surrounds me, In that Love I safely dwell, 'Tis a-
2. God is Life; that Life surrounds me, In that Life I safely dwell, 'Tis a-
f 3. God is health; that health surrounds me, In that health I safely dwell, 'Tis a-
p 4. God is peace; that peace surrounds me, In that peace I safely dwell, 'Tis a-

bove, beneath, with-in me, Love is mine. and all is well. God is
bove, beneath, with-in me, Life is mine, and all is well. God is
bove, beneath, with-in me, Health is mine, and all is well. God is
bove, beneath, with-in me, Peace is mine, and all is well. God is

In strict time to the close.   *fs p*

Love, pure Love, God is Love, sweet Love, That Love is mine—*mine*, and all is well.
Life, pure Life, God is Life, sweet Life, That Life is mine—*mine*, and all is well.
Health, pure Health, God is Health, sweet Health, That Health is mine—*mine*, and all is well.
Peace, pure Peace, God is Peace, sweet Peace, That Peace is mine—*mine*, and all is well.

f 5. God is Strength, etc.   7. God is Joy, etc.
    6. God is Light, etc.   8. God is Truth, etc.

WE'LL BE COMRADES.

H. S. L.

H. S. Lowing.

1. We will vol - un- teer to fight For our Lord, the Lord of Light, Who will
2. We will bat - tle for our Lord, With his Spir- it for our sword ; We will
3. Pressing onward in the fight, Pressing onward in the right, Precious

give his chosen peace and liber - ty ; Jesus Christ can never fail, He will
work and we will fight successful - ly : Nev- er can our efforts fail, Tho' the
laurels shall be ours for-ev - er- more ; Glo- ry to the Prince of Peace; Praise his

lead, tho' Sa - tan rail, He will lead us on to glorious vic - to - ry.
en - e - my prevail, We shall gain the last and fi - nal vic - to - ry.
name for our release ; Praise, O praise him on that ev - er- last- ing shore.

Chorus.

We'll be com - - - rades, We'll be comrades, When the bugle sounds the
Yes, we'll be com - rades,

glorious ju - bi - lee; We'll be com - - - rades, We'll be
ju - bi - lee; Yes, we'll be comrades,

com - rades When the vic - to - ry o'er sin has made us free.
made us free.

ADORATION.

JOHN BOWRING.

GEO. C. HUGG.

Maestoso.

1. How sweetly flowed the Gospel's sound, From lips of gentle- ness and grace,
2. From heav'n he came, of heav'n he spoke, To heav'n he led his foll'wers' way;
3. "Come, wand'rers! to my Father's home, Come, all ye weary ones, and rest;"

When list'ning thousands gathered round, And joy and rev'rence fill'd the place.
Dark clouds of gloomy night he broke, Unveiling an im - mor- tal day.
Yes, sacred Teacher; we will come, Obey thee, love thee, and be blest.

WHO'S FOR HIM?

WILLIAM HUGHES.

V. PAUL JONES.

1. Let us all stand up to-geth-er in the cause of Christ our King,
2. Let us all for him be fear-less, as we march up-on the foe,
3. Let us one and all then take our stand for Christ, our King, to-day,
4. Do not fal-ter in the con-flict, do not lin-ger by the way,

Fighting in the ranks of Je - sus; As we go in-to the
Fighting in the ranks of Je - sus; If we fol-low where he
Fighting in the ranks of Je - sus; And the spoils of vic-to-
Fighting in the ranks of Je - sus; For our Great Commander

bat-tle let us all his praises sing, Fighting in the ranks of Je-sus.
leads us, on to vic-to-ry we'll go, Fighting in the ranks of Je-sus.
ry at Je-sus' feet we soon will lay, Fighting in the ranks of Je-sus.
leads us on the bat-tle-field to-day, Fighting in the ranks of Je-sus.

CHORUS.

Who's for him? Who's for him? Who will sing the sto-ry, Stand for Christ and glory?

Who's for him? Who's for him? Stand up in the line for Je - sus.

Geo. C. Hugg.   Geo. C. Hugg.

1. In the morn of morns when we all meet there, In the home far above the sky;
2. Never sadness there, neither grief, nor tear, In that fair shining home on high!
3. With our kindred dear, in that love-light clear, While the long rolling ages fly,

We'll rehearse the scenes we have left behind, But we never will say "good-bye."
But they swell the song, happy ransomed throng; And they never will say "good-bye."
We will meet, and greet, at the Saviour's feet, But we never will say "good-bye."

CHORUS.

In the dawn - ing of the morn - ing, In that home far a-bove the sky;
In the dawning clear of the morning fair,

Hap-py meet - ing, hap-py greet - ing, When we never say "good-bye."
Happy meeting there, hap-py greeting there,

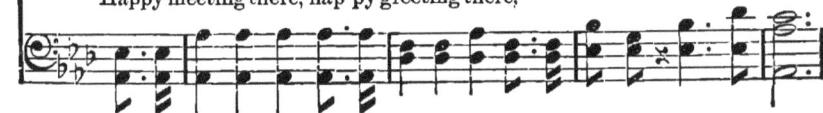

HE HIDETH MY SOUL.

Fanny J. Crosby.   Wm. J. Kirkpatrick.

Allegretto.

1. A won-derful Saviour is Je-sus my Lord, A won-derful Saviour to
2. A won-derful Saviour is Je-sus my Lord, He tak-eth my burden a-
3. With numberless blessings each moment he crowns, And filled with his fulness di-
4. When clothed in his brightness transported I rise To meet him in clouds of the

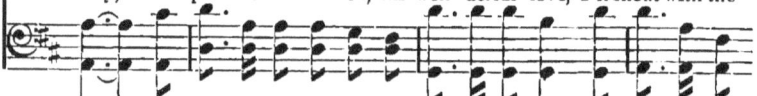

me,   He hid-eth my soul in the cleft of the Rock, Where riv-ers of
way,   He hold-eth me up, and I shall not be moved, He giv-eth me
vine, I sing in my rapture, O glo-ry to God For such a Re-
sky,   His per-fect sal-vation, his won-derful love, I'll shout with the

CHORUS.

pleasure I   see.
strength as my day.   } He hid-eth my soul in the cleft of the Rock, That
deem-er as   mine.
millions on   high.

shadows a dry, thirsty land; He hid-eth my life in the depths of his

love, And covers me there with his hand,   And covers me there with his hand.

Copyright, 1890, by Wm. J. Kirkpatrick.

NOTHING TO PAY.

F. R. HAVERGAL.
Slowly.

GEO. C. HUGG.

1. Nothing to pay! Ah; nothing to pay! Never a word of ex-cuse to say,
2. Nothing to pay! The debt is so great; What will you do with the awful weight?
3. Nothing to pay! Yes, nothing to pay! Jesus has clear'd all the debt a-way,

Year after year thou hast fill'd the score, Owing the Lord still more and more.
How shall the way of es-cape be made? Nothing to pay, yet all must be paid.
Blotted it out with His bleeding hand! Free and forgiv'n and loved you stand.

CHORUS.
Faster.

Hear......... the voice of Je-sus say, Ver-i-ly thou hast noth-ing to pay!
Hear......... the voice of Je-sus say, Ver-i-ly thou hast noth-ing to pay!
Hear......... the voice of Je-sus say, Ver-i-ly thou hast noth-ing to pay!

Ru-ined now, lost art thou, and yet I for-gave thee all thy debt.
All is charged to my own ac-count, I have paid the full a-mount.
Paid, the debt, and the debt-or's free! Now, I ask thee, "lov'st thou Me?"

HE NEVER WILL FORSAKE ME.

Jesse P. Tompkins.　　　　　Wm. J. Kirkpatrick.

1. Je - sus is mine, he nev - er will forsake me, Je - sus is
2. Je - sus is mine, he nev - er will deceive me, Je - sus is
3. Je - sus is mine, he nev - er will de - sert me, Je - sus is
4. Je - sus is mine, he nev - er will re - ject me, Je - sus is

mine, no e - vil can o'ertake me; I seek his kind - ly face, I
mine, his words shall nev - er grieve me; I know his love is true, And
mine, no grief can ev - er hurt me; For on his throbbing breast I
mine, his blood will e'er pro - tect me; And when be - fore the throne, I

trust him for his grace, O no, he nev - er will for - sake me.
what he says, he'll do, O no, he nev - er will de - ceive me.
can most sweet - ly rest, O no, he nev - er will de - sert me.
shall not stand a - lone, O no, he nev - er will re - ject me.

Chorus.

No, no, no, he nev - er will for - sake me, No, no, no, no
No, no, no, he nev - er will de - ceive me, No, no, no, his
No, no, no, he nev - er will de - sert me, No, no, no, no
No, no, no, ne nev - er will re - ject me, No, no, no, his

e - vil can o'er-take me ; His love will ev - er last, Till
words shall nev - er grieve me ; I know his love is true, And
grief can ev - er hurt me ; For on his throbbing breast I
blood will e'er pro - tect me ; And when be - fore his throne, I

all of earth is past, O no, he nev - er will for - sake me.
what he says, he'll do, O no, he nev - er will de - ceive me.
can most sweetly rest, O no, he nev - er will de - sert me.
shall not stand a - lone, No, no, he nev - er will re - ject me.

JESUS NEAR.

Dedicated to Wharton Street M. E. Sunday-school.

WM. H. CLARK.   POWELL G. FITHIAN.

Tenderly.

1. Jesus is near, so near, so near, His presence doth my Spir - it cheer ;
2. Jesus is near, so near, so near, He speaks and scatters ev - 'ry fear ;
3. Jesus is near, so near, so near, His love supreme dries ev - 'ry tear ;
4. Jesus is near, so near, so near, It doth not yet to us ap - pear

His gracious voice makes me re - joice To find him near, so near.........
I see his face, I taste his grace, For he is near, so near.........
Each burden bears, for me he cares, And holds me near, so near.........
What we shall be, but we shall see When Jesus comes so near.........

so near.

WILLIAM HUGHES.   V. PAUL JONES.

VOICES IN UNISON.

1. Je- sus will save us! Tell the glad story, Tell how he suffered and died ;
2. Je- sus will save us! Free us from bondage, Save us from sin and its shame ;
3. Je- sus will save us! Sweet is the telling, Dear was the ransom he gave ;
4. Je- sus will save us! Soon with the others Gathered in heaven we'll meet ;

How in his pit - y, in - fi - nite pit - y, On the cross was cru - ci - fied.
O what a blessing, sweet the confessing, Tell it out with joy a - gain.
Over the world the song still is swelling, Jesus triumphed o' er the grave.
O with what rapture we'll give him glory, Kneeling at his bless- ed feet.

CHORUS.

Jesus will save us ! Jesus will save us ! Cleanse us without and within ;..........

O what a glory, Sing loud the story, Jesus will save us from sin.........

HER SAILS ARE SPREAD FOR GLORY.

REV. JOHNSON OATMAN, JR.   REV. S. M. VANSANT.

1. My soul keeps sing-ing all day long, One sweet, one bless-ed sto - ry;
2. Our par-ents on this same ship sail'd, We've heard them tell the sto - ry;
3. This ship has car-ried mil-lions o'er, Her sails with age are hoar - y;
4. I'll meet you on the oth - er side, Where we'll talk o'er the sto - ry;

I'm on a ship which ne'er goes wrong, Whose sails are spread for glo - ry.
And how the Cap-tain nev - er fail'd, To bring all safe to glo - ry.
But there is room for million's more, O come and sail for glo - ry.
Of how we cross'd life's o - cean wide, And land - ed all in glo - ry.

CHORUS.

It's hal - le - lu - jah all the way, O sing and shout the sto - ry;

I'm on the good old ship to - day, Her sails are spread for glo - ry.

ARMY OF SALVATION.

Mrs. Frank A. Breck.   Powell G. Fithian.

1. Arm - y of sal - va - tion, hear the trumpet call; Go ye forth to
2. Arm - y of sal - va - tion, con - quer! for ye must Fight till sin is
3. Arm - y of sal - va - tion, let thy fears be o'er; Smite where heroes

bat - tle, break sin's mighty wall! Crowns and thrones must perish, kings and kingdoms fall,
vanquished, buried in the dust; Right shall be triumphant, God is true and just;
nev - er dared to smite be - fore: Christ shall reign in glo - ry, doubt it nevermore;

Chorus.

Till is crowned our Christ, the Saviour, "Lord of all."
In his pow'r the great Almight- y ye may trust.   } Forward! forward!
All the world shall own him Saviour, and a - dore.

heed the bat - tle cry; Hail sal - vation's ban - ner; lift the standard high;

Forward! forward! fighting till ye die, Ye shall gain the victo- ry by and by.

Arr. by GEO. C. HUGG.

GEO. C. HUGG.

Spirited.

1. O my sweet home, Je - ru - sa - lem! Thy joys when shall I see?
2. Thy gar - dens and thy good - ly walks, Con-tin - ual- ly are green,
3. Right thro' thy streets with pleasing sound, The flood of life doth flow;
4. O Moth - er dear, Je - ru - sa - lem! When shall I come to thee?

The King that sit - teth on thy throne, In His fe - lic - i - ty?
Where grow such sweet and pleasant flowers, As no-where else are seen.
And on the banks, on eith - er side, The trees of life do grow.
When shall my sor - rows have an end? Thy joys when shall I see.

CHORUS.

Way o - ver Jor - dan! Way o - ver Jor - dan! O

land of rest, and bliss un-told, My own e - ter - nal home.

WM. K. FISHER.   Matthew 8 : 27.   THOS. O'NEIL.

With reverence.

1. "What manner of man is this," This man on Gal - i - lee?
2. "What manner of man is this," Who tells the lame to walk,
3. "What manner of man is this," Who is a riv - er free,
4. "What manner of man is this," Who is the Liv - ing Bread
5. "What manner of man is this," Who'll save if we but look,

He speaks, and lo! he is obeyed, E'en by the wind and sea! E'en
And bids the deaf to hear the news, And e'en the dumb to talk? And
And all who drink, O glorious tho't! Shall nev - er thirst- y be? Shall
That sat - is- fies the hun- gry soul, And rais - es e'en the dead? And
And take from us our sin and woe, As writ - ten in the Book? As

slow.   CHORUS. *a tempo.*

by the wind and sea.
e'en the dumb to talk.
nev - er thirsty be.
rais- es e'en the dead.
writ- ten in the Book.
} He is the Babe of Bethlehem, The Rose of Sharon,

slow.

fair; The meek and low- ly Naz - a-rene, With whom none can compare!

HOMEWARD BOUND

HORATIUS BONAR.

GEO. C. HUGG.

1. This is not my place of rest-ing, Mine's a cit - y yet to come;
2. In it all is light and glo - ry, O'er it shines a nightless day;
3. There the Lamb, our Shepherd, leads us, By the streams of life a - long;
4. Soon we pass this des-ert drea-ry, Soon we bid fare-well to pain;

Onward to it I am hasting, On to my e - ter-nal home.
Ev-'ry trace of sin's sad sto - ry, All the curse has passed a - way.
On the fresh-est pas-tures feeds us, Turns our sigh-ing in - to song.
Nev-er more be sad and wea-ry, Nev-er more to sin a - gain.

CHORUS.

Homeward bound! homeward bound! Praise the Lord I'm homeward bound!
Homeward bound! homeward bound!

Mine is yon ce - les-tial cit - y, Praise the Lord I'm homeward bound.

CLIMBING UP THE MOUNTAIN.

Rev. Johnson Oatman, Jr.

Geo. C. Hugg.

1. Once I wandered in the val-ley, far be-low the mountain's crest,
2. Now no more I grope in darkness, for I'm liv-ing in the light;
3. Just a-head the pearl gates o-pen, and the walls of jas-per shine,
4. Now the world is far be-low me, I am on the Mount of God,

Then I had no place of safe-ty, then no sure, a-bid-ing rest;
I have found a pre-cious Saviour, who has scattered all my night;
While by faith I see a mansion which the Sav-iour says is mine;
And I tread where saints and an-gels of the a-ges past have trod;

But one day I caught a vis-ion of the day-star from on high,
I have found a lov-ing Fath-er, who can hear his children cry,
And I see my dear ones waiting, hear them shout, as I draw nigh,
Just a few more days of toil-ing, 'twill be o-ver by and by,

Then I start-ed up the mountain to that land beyond the sky.
And he helps me up the mountain toward that home beyond the sky.
"Climb on, climb on up the mountain to your home beyond the sky."
Then I'll rest up-on the mountain in that land beyond the sky.

Chorus.

Yes, I'm climbing, climbing, climbing up the moun - tain,
mountain, climbing,

Climbing up the Mount of God, that reach - es to the sky;

Yes, I'm climb - ing, climb - ing, climb - ing toward the sum - mit,

And by Je - sus' help I'll reach it, by and by.

JUST A WORD FOR MY REDEEMER.

H. S. L. Romans 10: 10. H. S. Lowing.

1. Just a word for my Redeem - er, Who has been so kind and true;
2. Just a word for my Redeem - er, Tho' the path be dark and drear;
3. Just a word for my Redeem - er, To a dark and doubting soul;
4. Just a word for my Redeem - er, Lov-ing words are sure to win;

Can I be so cold and thoughtless, While there's much that I can do?
It will point a soul to heav - en, And the clouds will dis - ap- pear.
It will give sweet peace and comfort, While the pass - ing moments roll.
Christ will crown our fee - ble ef - forts, Give us vic - t'ry o - ver sin.

CHORUS.

Just a word.............. may help an - oth - er,.......
Just a word may help an - oth - er, help an- oth - er,

Just a word.............. may save a broth - er;......
Just a word may save a broth - er, save a brother;

Just a word.......... may be a jew - el,......
Just a word may be a jew - el, be a jew - el,

In the sweet by......... and by.
by and by.

GOD OF LOVE.

Charles Wesley.   Geo. C. Hugg.

1. God of love, who hear- est prayer, Kindly for thy peo- ple care,
2. Save us, in the prosp'rous hour, From the flatt'ring tempter's pow'r,
3. Save us from the great and wise, Till they sink in their own eyes,
4. Nev- er let the world break in, Fix a migh ty gulf between;
5. Let us still to thee look up, Thee, thy Israel's strength and hope,

Who on thee a - lone de - pend: Love us, save us to the end.
From his un - sus - pect - ed wiles, From the world's per - ni - cious smiles.
Tame - ly to thy yoke sub - mit, Lay their hon- or at thy feet.
Keep us lit - tle and un- known, Prized and loved by God a - lone.
Noth - ing know, or seek, be - side Je - sus, and him cru - ci - fied.

PARDONING LOVE.

Mrs. Frank A. Breck.   Powell G. Fithian.

1. I am so glad my Re-deem-er came Down from his kingdom a-
2. I am so glad that his grace is free, Glad there is nothing to
3. I am so glad Je-sus waits to bring Hope to the wea-ry and

bove, A bless-ed sal-va-tion for all to pro-claim, And
pay; I'm glad that sal-va-tion is of-fered to me, And
sad, That all who will own him as Sav-iour and King In

CHORUS.

show us his par-don-ing love.
I have full par-don to - day. } Par-don-ing love is
par-don-ing love shall be glad.

free, is free; Par-don-ing love is wide, Par-don-ing

love reaches sinners like me, And reaches the world be - side.

HORATIUS BONAR.
JOHN GOSS.

1. Ban - ner of the bless - ed tree, Round its glo - ry gath - er ye!
2. King of glo - ry, Thee a - lone; King of kings, Thy name we own!
3. Spare not toil, nor blood, nor pain, Not a stroke de-scends in vain;

War - riors of the crown and cross, What is earth - ly gain or loss?
With thy ban - ners o - ver head Not ten thousand foes we dread.
Wound-ed, still no foot we yield On this blood-stained bat-tle field.

CHORUS.

More than conquerors e - ven now, With the war-sweat on our brow,

On - ward o'er the well-marked road, March we as the host of God.

THE WONDERFUL STORY.

WM. K. FISHER.

THOS. O'NEIL.

1. Oh, have you heard the won-der-ful sto-ry, That tells of a
2. Oh, have you heard the won-der-ful sto-ry, The sweetest that
3. Oh, will you hear the won-der-ful sto-ry, And hear-ing, let
4. Af-ter you've heard the won-der-ful sto-ry, And bid the dear

Saviour who died? He came from a-bove, from the Fa-ther of love,
ev-er was told, That brings such a rest to the heart that's oppress-ed,
Je-sus save you? He now is wait-ing, but you must be willing,
Saviour come in, You'll tell the glad sto-ry, to him give the glo-ry,

CHORUS.

He came, yes, to be cru-ci-fied!
This bless-ed old sto-ry of old?
To let him your na-ture re-new.
That you have been pardoned from sin.

Blessed old sto-ry, oh,

bless-ed old sto-ry! Tho' old, it is always more new; 'Tis a

wonder, oh, yes, this marvelous sto-ry—I love it because it is true!

MARCHING ON FOR JESUS.

"Thanks be to God, which giveth us the victory through our Lord Jesus Christ."—I. Cor. 15: 57.

Roy E. Mooar.   Geo. C. Hugg.

1. In God's name for - ward march - ing, A no - ble Christian band,
2. To Christ their great Re - deem - er, The ran - som'd arm - y sings,
3. Their watchword high En - deav - or, They stead - fast march a - long,

Is go - ing on vic - to - rious, And conquering ev - 'ry land;
The Church which He has plant - ed, Her choic - est off - 'ring brings;
The Fa - ther watch - es o'er them, The Spir - it makes them strong;

A glo - rious cause in - spires them, A glo - rious lead - er He,
Great was the love that sought them, While wand'ring lost in sin;
They go to spread sal - va - tion, And bring the prom-ised day,

Who leads them on to con - flict, And on to vic - to - ry.
They praise the Lord who bought them, And called them un - to Him.
When ev - 'ry land and na - tion, Shall own the Sav-iour's sway.

MY GAZE IS FIXED ON JESUS.

Rev. Johnson Oatman, Jr.

Powell G. Fithian.

1. While trav'ling thro' this vale of tears, My gaze is fixed on Je - sus;
2. Let world-ly cares and woes increase, My gaze is fixed on Je - sus;
3. When waves of trou - ble stretch ahead, My gaze is fixed on Je - sus;
4. I'll tell the world, where'er I'm led, My gaze is fixed on Je - sus;

By day or night I have no fears, My gaze is fixed on Je - sus.
I find in him the Prince of Peace, My gaze is fixed on Je - sus.
Where'er he leads I'll safe - ly tread, My gaze is fixed on Je - sus.
I'll sing up - on my dy - ing bed, My gaze is fixed on Je - sus.

CHORUS.

Christ Je - sus is my dear- est friend; I'll ev'rywhere his love commend;

I'll fol - low him un - to the end; My gaze is fixed on Je - sus.

BROTHER TURN YOUR FOOTSTEPS HOMEWARD. 41

IDA L. REED.   ADAM GEIBEL.

1. Broth-er turn thy foot-steps homeward, For the 'ev - en-tide draws nigh;
2. Broth-er turn thy foot-steps homeward, Long thy Lord hath plead with thee;
3. Broth-er turn thy foot-steps homeward, Youthful days be-hind thee lie;
4. Broth-er turn thy foot-steps homeward, Still thy Fa - ther waits for thee;

Twi-light shades will soon be fall-ing, And the stars shine in the sky.
But thou wouldst not hear or heed Him, And too late it soon may be.
Lift thine eyes to heav-en's glo - ry, Ere the night of death draws nigh.
Soon life's gates may close up-on it, Vain would then thy pleadings be.

CHORUS.

Broth-er turn your foot-steps homeward, Do not long - er i - dly wait;

For the hours of day are o - ver, Soon will close life's gold- en gate.

JESUS DIED FOR YOU.

WM. B. WILLIAMS.   POWELL G. FITHIAN.

1. On Calv'ry's cross the Saviour died That we may be saved from sin ;
2. O   sinner, now, while life is yours, Cling to   your sins no   more,
3. And then by faith, and faith a- lone, Lay   off   thy guilt and shame ;

That by his blood, his precious blood, We may be cleansed with - in.
But press your way to Je - sus' side ; He's called you o'er and o'er.
Be- lieve his blood will cleanse from sin And break sin's strongest chain.

CHORUS.

Cleansed with - in   by grace di - vine, From sin   en - tire - ly   free ;

Now go thy way to per - fect day ; His blood was shed for   thee.

IT'S BETTER ON THE OTHER SIDE.

Rev. Johnson Oatman, Jr.   Adam Geibel.

1. Tho' days may be se - rene and bright, Yet quickly falls the shades of night;
2. Death en - ters in our cir-cles here, And robs us of our friends so dear;
3. Here pride divides the rich and poor, And causes wrongs hard to en-dure;
4. In that blest land no tears will fall, No hearts will ache, no fears ap-pall;
5. Our Fa-ther owns that bless-ed land, Our broth-ers lead us by the hand;

But just be-yond life's roll-ing tide, It's bet-ter on the oth-er side.
But there, He can - not friends divide, It's bet-ter on the oth-er side.
But in that land there is no pride, It's bet-ter on the oth-er side.
No mat-ter here what may be-tide, It's bet-ter on the oth-er side.
With them we ev - er will a-bide, When we have reach'd the oth-er side.

CHORUS.

The oth - er side, how wondrous fair, All bright and glorious o - ver there;

When we have cross'd life's rolling tide, It's bet - ter on the oth - er side.

THE COMING OF HIS FEET.

Rev. Johnson Oatman, Jr.

Geo. C. Hugg.

1. In God's ho - ly Word 'tis written That our Lord will come a - gain;
2. Oft I wan-der in the shadows, Oft the path is out of sight,
3. Tho' I'm called to pass the val - ley And the shadow of the dead,

He will come to earth to judge it, Not to suf - fer death or pain.
But I hear a sweet voice call- ing, "Fol- low me, 'twill soon be light."
He has promised to be with me, So of them I have no dread.

He will summon all the faithful In the air their Lord to meet,
He has promised when in dan- ger To pro- vide a safe re - treat,
"I'll be with you," is the promise At that hour I will re - peat,

So I'm watching night and morning For the com- ing of his feet.
So I've learned to watch thro' darkness For the com- ing of his feet.
And while dy- ing, I will list - en For the com- ing of his feet.

CHORUS.

I am wait - - ing, I am watch - - ing,
I am waiting, yes, I'm waiting, I am watching, yes, I'm watching,

Yes, I'm watching for my Saviour's face so sweet;
so sweet;

I am wait - - ing, I am watch - - ing,
I am waiting night and morning, I am watching night and morning,

I am wait-ing for the com-ing of his feet.
his feet.

SAFELY SHELTERED IN THE SAVIOUR'S LOVE.

J. L. Newkirk.   Chas. A. McCormick.

1. Safe - ly sheltered in the Saviour's love, From all dan - ger
2. As we jour - ney o'er the stream of life, Dark and storm - y
3. Safe - ly sheltered, now our prais - es sing, No more dan - ger,

there I will a - bide; When the storm-clouds gath - er on the way,
oft may be the way; But our Sav - iour, ev - er at the helm,
all the storms are past; Je - sus, Sav - iour, thou hast paid the price,

CHORUS.

He will keep me ev - er by 'his side.)
Speaks one word, the waves and storms o- bey. } He.......... will keep me
Thro' thy blood we're safe- ly home at last.) He will keep me

by his side, From........ all dan - ger he will hide; The cleansing
             From all dan - ger

wave that flows from Cal - va - ry Cleanses me, yes, e - ven me.
                                                    even me.

THE SHELTERING ROCK.

ISAIAH 32: 2. 12: 3. 65: 10. COL. 1: 20.

W. E. PENN.

W. E. PENN.

Slow. May be sung with good effect as a Solo.

1. There is a Rock in a wea-y land, Its shad-ow falls on the
2. There is a Well in a des-ert plain, Its wa-ters call with en-
3. A great fold stands with its por-tals wide, The sheep a-stray on the
4. There is a cross where the Sav-iour died, His blood flow'd out in a

burn-ing sand, In-vit-ing pil-grims as they pass To seek a
treat-ing strain, "Ho, ev-'ry thirst-ing sin-sick soul, Come, free-ly
mount-ain side, The Shepherd climbs o'er mountains steep, He's searching
crim-son tide A sac-ri-fice for sins of men, And free to

REFRAIN.

shade in the wil-der-ness.
drink, and thou shalt be whole."
now for His wand'ring sheep.
all who will en-ter in.

Then why will ye die? Oh! why will ye die?

Slower.

When the shelt'ring Rock is so near by?
When the liv-ing Well is so near by?
When the Shepherd's fold is so near by?
When the crim-son cross is so near by?

Oh! why will ye die?

"MY WAYWARD BOY, I LOVE YOU STILL."

Solo, Baritone or Mezzo Soprano.

Rev. John L. Newkirk.   Powell G. Fithian.

Andante. Tenderly.

1. How sad the day, when but a youth, Cheerful and gay, I oft did
2. I wandered on, yet further on, In-to the path of sin and
3. Oh, bless his name, he heard my cry, And at his feet I humbly

roam; Then soon my heart by sin was turned From the hearth-
woe; Oft when the nights were cold and bleak I had no
bow; His pre-cious blood o'er me does flow, He saves me

stone and from the home. How moth-'er dear was bowed with
home, no where to go. Then came to me, on mem'ry's
now, yes, saves me now. Some day to heav'n, I'll meet her

grief,   And anx - ious care   her soul did   fill,   "Tho' wand'ring
wall,   How oft   I   sat   at   mother's   knee;   And she would
there,   And ev - er thro'   e - ter - ni - ty   Will praise his

far,   my boy," she said, "I'll love you still,   yes, love you still."
sing   of Je - sus' love; But does he care   for one like me?
name   for one who said, "Tho' wand'ring far,   I still love thee."

CHORUS.

Yet oft the home in visions comes, And mother's voice would bring a thrill

With much pathos.

p

When sweetly she would seem to say, "My wayward boy, I love you still."

50 THERE'S NO LOVE LIKE HIS LOVE TO ME.

John L. Newkirk.   (Solo or Duet.)   Powell G. Fithian.

With tenderness.

1. There's no love to me like the love of Je - sus, Ev - er, al - ways
2. When far, far a - way, and in con - dem - na - tion, Feel - ing no one
3. Oh, won - der - ful love, is the love of Je - sus, Who on Cal - v'ry's

just the same; E'en tho' of this world you may be most low - ly,
cared for me, There came a sweet voice, I shall ne'er for - get it,
cru - el tree Was wounded and died to make full a - tone - ment

CHORUS.

Je - sus still loves you, bless his name.
"Je - sus thy Sav - iour still loves thee."   There nev - er was
For a poor sin - ner, lost, like me.

one like Je - sus, Ev - er, al - ways true is he; There never was

one like Je - sus, There's no love like his love to me.

TELL THE STORY OF HIS LOVE.

REV. G. MURRAY KLEPFER.   J. M. BLACK.

1. Tell the won - der - ful sto - ry of Je - sus; How from
2. Would you light - en the hearts that are hea - vy? Drive the
3. There is full - ness of joy in His pres - ence, There is

glo - ry to earth He came; How He suffered and died to re-deem us;
clouds from the darkened skies? Tell the sto - ry of grace all-suf - fi - cient,
peace for the rec - on - ciled, Un - to those who believe He is pre-cious,

CHORUS.

How He lives ev - er-more the same. ⎫ Tell the sto - - ry of His
And the strength which His love supplies. ⎬ Tell the sto - ry,
Ev - er near to the trust-ing child. ⎭

love, Spread the ti - dings far and near, Tell the
of Je-sus' love, far and near,

sto - - ry of His love, Tell it out that the world may hear.
Tell the sto-ry of Jesus' love,

Copyright, 1894, by J. M. Black.

WHEN IN TROUBLE.

W. H. CLARK.

POWELL G. FITHIAN.

1. There's One to whom I'll sure-ly go, Tho' adverse winds may fiercely blow;
2. So in the midst of worldly care I'll pour my heart to him in prayer;

Tho' tempests, ris-ing wild and high, Obscure the face of yonder sky.
And he who sees a sparrow fall Will kind-ly list-en when I call.

His voice controls the winds and waves; His outstretched hand the sink-ing
And he who sits up-on the throne Will nev-er leave me all a

saves; My bark the storm cannot o'erwhelm While Jesus' hand is-on the helm.
lone, But gen-tly lead me by his hand, To heav'n's own pure and bet-ter land.

W. S.

WM. STONE.

1. The Sav-iour is call-ing, child come home, No long-er in dark-ness roam;
2. You've wasted so ma-ny pre-cious years, O cease from thy sin-ful way;
3. There's nothing to gain, why thus de-lay, The pleas-ures of life are vain;

I've gone to pre-pare a place for thee, O wan-der-ing child come home.
And hast-en to greet a Saviour's love, His par-don-ing voice o-bey.
Come drink at the fount of joy and peace, And thou shalt live a-gain.

CHORUS.

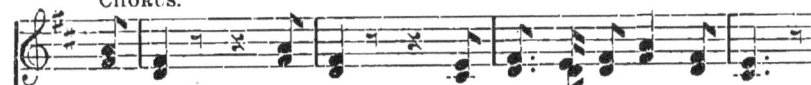

Come home, come home, O wan-der-ing child come home;
my child, my child,

'Tis Je-sus in-vites you, why longer roam, O wan-der-ing child come home.

"COME UNTO ME."

William Hughes.

V. Paul Jones.

1. "Come un - to me." These words, so soft - ly spok - en, Fell from the lips of
2. "Come un - to me." Will you re - sist his calling? Will you repulse that
3. "Come un - to me." Must he for - ev - er call thee? Think of the death he

Je- sus, long a - go. "Come un - to me." The silence still seems broken
ten- der, lov- ing plea? Come 'neath the drops that from his side are fall- ing;
died for you and me! Think of the pain and anguish he has suffered,

D. S.—"Come un - to me." With thee his voice is pleading,

rit.   *Fine.*   Chorus.

By that same voice, so full of pain and woe.)
Bathe in the blood; 'twill cleanse and comfort thee. } Hark! hark! hark! O
Nailed to the cross and crowned in mock- er - y!)

Sweet - ly it calls thee, weary wand'rer, home.

D.S.

sinner, give thou heeding, Do not lin - ger! Do not longer roam!

THE EVERLASTING ARMS.

REV. E. A. HOFFMAN.

A. J. SHOWALTER.

1. What a fel - low-ship, what a joy di - vine, Lean - ing
2. Oh, how sweet to walk in this pil - grim way, Lean - ing
3. What have I to do, what have I to fear, Lean - ing

on the Ev - er - last - ing Arms! What a bless - ed - ness,
on the Ev - er - last - ing Arms! Oh, how bright the path
on the Ev - er - last - ing Arms! I have peace complete

what a peace is mine, Lean-ing on the Ev - er - last - ing Arms.
grows from day to day, Lean-ing on the Ev - er - last - ing Arms.
with my Lord so near, Lean-ing on the Ev - er - last - ing Arms.

CHORUS.

Lean - ing, lean - ing, Safe and se-cure from all a-larms;
Leaning on Je - sus, leaning on Je - sus,

Lean - ing, lean - ing, Lean-ing on the Ev - er-lasting Arms!
Leaning on Je - sus, leaning on Je - sus,

G. C. H.

GEO. C. HUGG.

Slowly and feelingly.

1. In the home com-ing of our King, We'll meet our
2. In the home com-ing of our King, We'll join the
3. In the home com-ing of our King, With Je - sus

loved ones gone be - fore, And sweet the greet-ing they will bring
ev - er - last-ing psalm Of joy, that an - gel voic - es sing,
we will live al - way, Where songs of love and glad-ness ring

CHORUS.

To us, up - on the blood-washed shore.
"The song of Mo - ses and the Lamb."
In tune, thro' heav'ns e - ter - nal day.
Happy home coming, Blessed

rit.   *a tempo.*

home coming, Glorious home com - ing of our Saviour, King! Happy

home coming, Blessed home coming, Glorious home coming of our Saviour, King!

IT'S FILLING ME.

Rev. Johnson Oatman, Jr.

Adam Geibel.

1. All a-round this ver-y hour, Falls there streams of heav'nly pow'r;
2. Send us show'rs of heav'nly grace, Let Thy pres-ence fill this place;
3. Thou a-lone this pow'r can'st give, With-out which I dare not live;

Fall-ing now so full and free, Praise the Lord, it's fill-ing me.
Speak the word and it shall be, That thy show-ers fall on me.
Give me pow'r to work for thee, Let the stream reach e-ven me.

CHORUS.

Hal-le-lu-jah! feel the pow'r, Fall-ing like a mighty show'r;

Com-ing now so full and free, Praise the Lord, it's fill-ing me.

I'M HOMESICK FOR HEAVEN TO-NIGHT.

(Solo and Chorus.)

Rev. Johnson Oatman, Jr.　　　　　　　　　　　Powell G. Fithian.

Andante moderato, with pathos.

1. The home of my childhood was cheer - ful and bright, For
2. I read in God's Word of a cit - y so fair, Whose
3. I read that my Sav - iour has gone to pre - pare A

fa - ther and moth - er were there ; Their love like a lamp filled my
Build - er and Mak - er is God ; No fam - ine or sor - row will
mansion in heav - en for me ; If I am but faith - ful, his

path - way with light, They ban - ished each shad - ow of
ev - er come there, Its streets by im - mor - tals are
glo - ry I'll share, And I my Re - deem - er shall

piu mosso.

care.

trod.

see.

But fa- ther and mother have gone from my side, They

They nev - er are sick in that beau- ti - ful land, No

I'll see all the scars he obtained on the tree, I'll

piu mosso.

a tempo.

live now in heaven's own light; I long to be with them, once

tears ev - er there dim the sight; So now as I think of that

gaze on his face with de- light; My spir - it looks upward, and

a tempo.

more to a- bide, I'm homesick for heaven to- night.

blest golden strand, I'm homesick for heaven to- night.

longs to be free, I'm homesick for heaven to- night.

VENITE AD ME.

UNKNOWN.

Matt. xi, 28-30.   Rev. xxii, 17.

1 COME unto me, all ye that labor and are | heavy- | laden, ‖ and | I will | give
    you | rest.
2 Take my yoke upon you, and learn of me; for I am meek and | lowly- -in |
    heart : ‖ and ye shall find | rest- -unto | your— | souls.
3 For my yoke is easy, and my | burden- -is | light, ‖ for my yoke is easy, | and
    my | burden- -is | light.
4 And the Spirit and the Bride say, Come. And let him that | heareth,- -say, |
    Come. ‖ And let him that is athirst come; and whosoever will, let him take
    the | water- -of | life— | freely. A- | men.

PROMPTLY, SWEETLY, GLADLY.

E. E. HEWITT.
ADAM GEIBEL.

(DUET.) *With feeling.*

1. Do kind things promptly; don't de-lay; The fleet-ing hours will nev-er
2. Do kind things sweet-ly; let the heart Be quick to learn love's winning
3. Do kind things glad-ly; blest em-ploy, To serve the King with songs of

stay For du-ties that we might have done, For vict'ries that we might have won.
art, To find the best, the kindest way Of helping oth-ers, day by day.
joy! When drawn from sparkling springs above, Our lives flow out in rills of love.

CHORUS.

Prompt-ly, prompt-ly   Then His

Prompt-ly, prompt-ly "in His name,"

prom - ise

Then His prom-ise we may claim, Then His wel - come word will

Then His welcome

un - to me."

be, "Ye have done it, done it un - to me."

LANDING ONE BY ONE.

This beautiful thought was suggested while returning home with a large Sunday-
school picnic on an excursion steamer. With songs of praise upborne
by children's voices, and the sun low in the heavens, we reached our
destination. The gangplank was pushed out, and one by one
they landed and disappeared in the streets of the city.

G. C. H.   GEO. C. HUGG.

Slowly and feelingly.

1. Safe on board the "Old Ship Zi - on," homeward bound, With glad
2. Trust - y helmsman, guide the "Old Ship" safe - ly home, Where no
3. What a meet- ing of the faith - ful that will be, On the

hal - le - lu - jahs ringing all a - round, Lo, the landing in the
lightning flash or tempest ev - er come; Guide us safe to yon - der
ver - nal banks, beyond the crys - tal sea! With the ransomed host to

distance I can see! Hal - le - lujah! hear them shout the vic - to - ry.
bright and ver - nal shore, Where we'll land, and dwell with loved ones ev - er- more.
join the glorious psalm, Aye, the new, new "Song of Moses and the Lamb."

CHORUS.

One by one, one by one, They are landing, at the
One by one, one by one,

setting of the sun, From the river's golden landing, where prophet's feet have

rall - en - tan - do.

trod, They're marching thro' the cit - y to the pal- ace of our God.

JESUS, TOUCH THIS HEART OF MINE.

WILLIAM HUGHES.　　　　　　　　　　　V. PAUL JONES.

1. Je-sus, touch this heart of mine With thy hallowed, sweet ca - ress;
2. Je-sus, ease me of my woe By thy gracious love di - vine;
3. Let me on - ly for thee live, And my lips thy prais- es sing;
4. Je-sus, take my will- ing hand, Guide me in thy hallowed way;

Draw me near thee, ne' er to part; Fill me with thy hap - pi - ness.
Naught of hap - pi - ness I'll know Till thou make me whol - ly thine.
Thee the glo - ry ev - er give, On - ly thee, my Sav - iour, King.
Lead me to the bet- ter land, To that brighter, end - less day.

Rev. Johnson Oatman, Jr.   Nehemiah 1: 11.   Powell G. Fithian.

1. I am a cup-bearer for Je-sus my King, I fill it with wa-ter from
2. To hous-es of mourning ofttimes I am led, Where grief and where sadness a-
3. A cup of forgiveness I oft pass a-long, A cup of forbearance with
4. A cup fill'd with hope ere life's last hour is spent, A cup fill'd with mercy for

God's living spring; Thro' this world where sor-row and sin doth a-bound, To
round me are spread; With sweet sym-pa-thy then my cup doth o'er-flow, And
those who do wrong; To those who need cheering o'er life's wea-ry mile, I
those who re-pent; A cup from the fountain of Cal-va-ry's tide, A

CHORUS.

all those in trouble I pass it around. ⎫
sheds a bright sunbeam in that house of woe. ⎪ A cup of sal-vation to
take them the king's cup fill'd with a glad smile. ⎬
cup of sal-vation, for Je-sus hath died. ⎭

those lost in sin, A cup fill'd with kindness some poor soul may win; O help us dear

Saviour where'r man is found, To take up the King's cup and pass it a-round.

HE CARETH FOR YOU.

IDA L. REED.   ADAM GEIBEL.

1. What tho' the days be drear-y, He cares, He cares for you;
2. Be brave the heavenly Fa-ther, Knows all that tries you here;
3. Then on His strong arm lean-ing, Go for-ward un-dis-may'd;
4. What e'er the days may bring thee, Know this He cares for thee;

O broth-er, worn and wea-ry, Let this thy strength re-new.
And tho' you walk in shad-ow, He's ev-er, ev-er near.
Fear not to brave life's per-ils, For He will give thee aid.
And tri-als oft bring bless-ings, And mer-cies rich and free.

CHORUS.

For you, for you He car-eth, And tri-als by and by,

Will all be lost in tri-umphs, And joys that can-not die.

THE ANGELS FROM GLORY.

Rev. Johnson Oatman, Jr.

Geo. C. Hugg.

1. My Saviour has gone to prepare me a home, A beau - ti - ful
2. Tho' struggles and hardships I meet on the way, The journey of
3. When Sa - tan and sin seem to har - ass my soul, If waves of af-
4. So, I will keep singing, while passing a - long, For soon I will

mansion a - bove yon blue dome ; And when from this bod - y my
life will be o - ver some day ; Then if I at last with the
flic - tion a - bove me shall roll, I know when God o - pens a
join in the glo - ri - fied song ; And when I look upward through

soul is set free, The an - gels from glo - ry are com - ing for me.
faithful shall be, The an - gels from glo - ry are com - ing for me.
path thro' the sea ; The an - gels from glo - ry are com - ing for me.
faith I can see The an - gels from glo - ry are com - ing for me.

CHORUS.

Coming for me, yes, com - ing for me, The an - gels from

glo - ry are com - ing for me; Just o - ver life's troubles and

sorrows I see The an - gels of glo - ry are com - ing for me.

5

DUNDEE. C. M.

JOSEPH ADDISON.   GUILLAUME FRANC.

1. When all thy mer - cies, O my God, My ris - ing soul sur - veys,
2. O how can words with e - qual warmth The grat - i - tude de - clare
3. Thro' all e - ter - ni - ty to thee A grate - ful song I'll raise;

Transport - ed with the view I'm lost In won - der, love and praise.
That glows with - in my ravished heart? But thou canst read it there.
But O, e - ter - ni - ty's too short To ut - ter all thy praise.

I'M GLAD THAT JESUS CAME.

Rev. Johnson Oatman, Jr.

Powell G. Fithian.

1. The Lord came down to die for me, To die a death of shame;
2. A sin - ner once, no hope had I, But doomed to end- less woe;
3. 'Twas love that brought the Sav-iour down, 'Twas love that made him die;
4. I'll praise him while he gives me breath, I'll praise his ho - ly name;

For me he hung up - on the tree, O glo - ry to his name!
But Je - sus heard my bit - ter cry, Because he loved me so.
'Twas love prepared the robe and crown, To give us by and by.
I'll sing in heav - en, af - ter death, "I'm glad that Je - sus came."

Chorus.

I'm glad that Je - sus died for me, I'm glad that Je - sus came;

He died for me up - on the tree, I'm glad that Je - sus came.

ARMY OF CHRIST.

T. J. POTTER. JOHNSON BARKER.

1. Brightly gleams our banner, Pointing to the sky, Waving wand'rers onward
2. Je-sus, Lord, and Master, At thy sa-cred feet, Here with hearts rejoicing,
3. All our days di-rect us, In the way we go, Lead us on vic-to-rious
4. Then with Saints and Angels May we join above, Offering end-less prais-es

To their home on high; Journeying o'er the desert, Glad-ly thus we pray,
See thy children meet; Oft-en have we left Thee, Oft-en gone a - stray,
O - ver ev-ery foe; Bid thine angel shield us, When the storm-clouds lower,
At thy throne of love; When the toil is o - ver, Then comes rest and peace,

CHORUS.

And with hearts united, Take our heav'n ward way.
Keep us, mighty Sav-iour, In the narrow way.
Pardon thou and save us In the last dread hour.
Je-sus, in his beauty;—Songs that never cease.

Brightly gleams our banner,

Point-ing to the sky, Waving wand'rers on-ward To their home on high.

COME INTO THE ARK.

Rev. Johnson Oatman, Jr.

Geo. C. Hugg.

Fervently.

1. For a hundred years or more, good old No - ah gave the warning,
2. But the wicked world went on, and they would not heed his cry - ing,
3. Time with us will soon be o'er, shades of night will soon be fall - ing,
4. Je - sus has prepared a place, and he will re - fuse you nev - er,

"Sin- ner, come in - to the ark ;   For the mighty winds will
"Sin- ner, come in - to the ark ;"   Till at last all hope was
Sin- ner, come in - to the ark ;   Hast- en to the o - pen
Sin- ner, come in - to the ark ;   He will save you by his
in - to the ark ;

roar, and the floods will come some morning,   Sinner, come in - to   the ark."
gone, in the waters they were dying,   Sinner, come in - to   the ark.
door, don't you hear the Saviour calling?   "Sinner, come in - to   the ark."
grace, list- en to his "whoso- ev - er,"   Sinner, come in - to   the ark.

CHORUS.

O   sin - ner, come in - to   the ark,   Dear sin - ner, come
in - to the ark ;

in - to the ark ; List - en to this note of warning,

in - to the ark ;

Do not wait an - oth - er morning, But sinner, come in - to the ark.

LISBON. S. M.

CHARLES WESLEY.

DANIEL READ.

1. And can I yet de - lay My lit - tle all to give?
2. Nay, but I yield, I yield; I can hold out no more :
3. Tho' late, I all for - sake; My friends, my all, re - sign :
4. Come, and pos - sess me whole, Nor hence a - gain re - move;

To tear my soul from earth a - way For Je - sus to re - ceive?
I sink, by dy - ing love compelled, And own thee con - quer - or.
Gracious Redeem - er, take, O take, And seal me ev - er thine.
Set - tle and fix my wav'ring soul With all thy weight of love.

I AM HIS, AND HE IS MINE.

Rev. Johnson Oatman, Jr.   Powell G. Fithian.

1. I once was bound with fet - ters, But now, thank God, I'm   free;
2. No more I walk in dark - ness, But, praise the Lord, I   see;
3. I'll tell the world a - bout him, Wher- ev - er I may   be;
4. I still will keep on sing - ing, Thro' all e - ter - ni - ty;

For I be- long to Je - sus, And he belongs to   me.

Chorus.

My soul is filled with sun - shine, I'm hap - py, light and   free;

For I be- long to Je - sus, And he belongs to   me.

ROLL HIS PRAISE ALONG.

Rev. Johnson Oatman, Jr.   J. Howard Entwisle.

1. Come all ye sons and daughters, And sing a hap - py song;
2. Sing prais-es to your Sav-iour, With voi-ces clear and strong;
3. With Je - sus as your Cap-tain, You nev-er will go wrong;
4. When you are faint and wea - ry, His arm is ev - er strong;
5. He'll take you home to Heav - en, To join that white-robed throng;

Christ Je - sus hath re-deem'd you, O roll His praise a - long.
He died for your sal - va - tion, O roll His praise a - long.
He'll lead you on to glo - ry, O roll His praise a - long.
He nev - er will for-sake you, O roll His praise a - long.
Where you will live for-ev - er, O roll His praise a - long.

CHORUS.

O come and sing for Je - sus, Let Him in-spire your song;

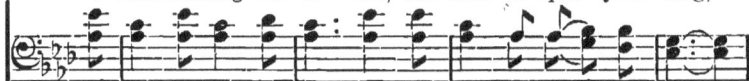

He is your on - ly ref - uge, O roll His praise a - long.

THE WEEPING OF THE NIGHT.

Rev. Johnson Oatman, Jr.

Geo. C. Hugg.

1. Are we walking un-der clouds and shadows here? There's a thought that should our
2. When the darkness of the night has passed away, With what happy hearts we
3. When our friends have whispered out this last farewell, O the sorrow of that
4. Soon the sorrows of this life will all be o'er, Soon we'll see the morning

onward pathway cheer : We would never know the joy at morning
sing and shout and pray ; Do the skies seem more than ev- er clear and
moment none can tell ; But we'll grasp their hands a- gain at morning
break on yon- der shore ; When we join that blessed throng, arrayed in
pathway cheer ;

light If it were not for the weeping of the night.
bright? This is ow- ing to the weeping of the night.
light, Where we'll nev - er know the weeping of the night.
white, We'll praise Je - sus for the weeping of the night.
of the night.

CHORUS.

O the weeping, precious weeping of the night, How we watch thro' tearful
of the night,

eyes for morning light; But we'd nev-er know the joy at dawning
morning light;

bright If it were not for the weeping of the night.
dawning bright of the night.

HORTON. 7.

XAVIER SCHNYDER VON WARTENSEE.

1. Light of lights, shine in my soul, Of my life il-lume the whole;
2. Send a gleam a-long the road I must trav-el hence to God;
3. Drive the darkness from my mind, May I, in thee, all things find;
4. Let thy cleansing ray di-vine Pu-ri-fy this life of mine;
5. So thine im-age, Lord, shall be Per-fect-ly wrought out in me;

Fill me on-ly with thy-self, From me cast out all things else.
Guide each step, and day by day Lead me thro' life's darkened way.
Dai-ly in my heart a-bide, Nothing shall I want be-side.
Take a-way the stain of sin, Make me white and clean within.
Like thee I shall then be-come, When thou tak'st thy servant home.

76 GONE ON.

REV. JOHNSON OATMAN, JR.

POWELL G. FITHIAN.

DUET.

1. Far, far above these scenes of night, To that blest land so fair and bright,
2. God has a mansion in the sky For all his children, when they die;
3. Where the redeemed for-ev - er sing, Where angels make their glad harps ring-
4. Where joy will last thro' endless years, Where nev- er cometh doubts and fears,
5. To that land by the crys- tal sea, Where with their Saviour they will be,

Where faith is swallowed up in sight, My fa - ther has gone on.
Up to her bless- ed home on high My moth - er has gone on.
With prais - es to their Lord and King, My broth - er has gone on.
Where God shall wipe a - way all tears, My sis - ter has gone on.
Hap - py thro' all e - ter - ni - ty, Our children have gone on.

CHORUS.

Gone on to that bright land so fair, Gone on beyond this world of care;

God help - ing me, I'll meet him there, My fa - ther has gone on.
God help - ing me, I'll meet her there, My moth- er has gone on.
God help - ing me, I'll meet him there, My broth- er has gone on.
God help - ing me, I'll meet her there, My sis - ter has gone on.
God help - ing us, we'll meet them there, Our children have gone on.

JESUS CAN HELP YOU, AND WILL.

REV. JOHNSON OATMAN, JR.   ADAM GEIBEL.

1. When trou - ble op - press you O do not des-pair, Tell Je - sus your
2. O soul far from Je - sus and burdened with sin, There's on - ly one
3. When loss - es take from you your sil-ver and gold, There's one who will
4. When life's sun is set - ing to rise here no more, There's on - ly one

trou - bles and give Him your care, He's prom - ised to meet you, when
way for the light to shine in, Ask Je - sus to help you and
give you His rich - es un - told, When those who once flat - tered seem
friend who can see you safe o'er, When flash - es the light from that

CHORUS.

of - fer- ing pray'r, Je - sus can help you, and will. ⎫
have faith in Him, Je - sus can help you, and will. ⎬ Je - sus can help you,
si - lent and cold, Je - sus can help you, and will. ⎭
ech - o - less shore, Je - sus can help you, and will.

Je - sus can help you, Je - sus can help you, and will—He will, Go

will.

to Him in pray'r, He'll always be there, Je - sus can help you and will, He will.

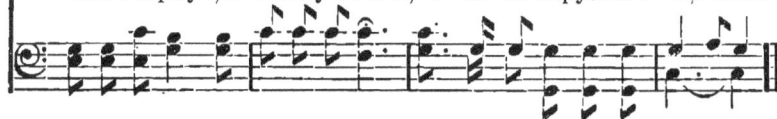

PRAISE THE LORD, I'LL BE THERE.

Rev. Johnson Oatman, Jr.

Geo. C. Hugg.

1. When we hear the trumpet sounding, on the res-ur-rec-tion day,
2. When the pearl-y gates swing o-pen to ad-mit the ransomed train
3. There will be a wedding sup-per in that mansion, by and by,
4. So a-mid the trials and dangers, that I meet on ev-'ry hand,

Call-ing us to meet our Saviour in the air; When the
To that bless-ed home where all is bright and fair; When the
When the Lamb will wed his Bride so spotless, fair; From all
I will put my trust in God, and not de-spair, For his
in the air;

seal of death is bro-ken, and the night has passed a-way; When his
great pro-ces-sion en-ters, with their Lord and King to reign; When they
na-tions they will gath-er to that banquet in the sky; But when
pre-cious Bi-ble tells me of a brighter, bet-ter land, And I

CHORUS.

peo-ple rise to meet him; I'll be there.
march around the cit-y; I'll be there.
ev-'rything is read-y, I'll be there.
know, when life is o-ver, I'll be there.

Praise the Lord, I'll be there, when the

saints and an - gels gath- er In that bright home in heaven, I'll be

there, I'll be there ; When we hear the Saviour say, "Come, ye blessed of my

Father, In - to mansions of glo- ry," I'll be there. I'll be there.

ST. THOMAS. S. M.

Isaac Watts, alt. by J. Wesley. Handel, arr. by Williams.

1. Come, ye that love the Lord, And let your joys be known ;
2. Let those re - fuse to sing, Who nev - er knew our God ;
3. Then let our songs a - bound, And ev - 'ry tear be dry :

Join in a song with sweet ac- cord, While ye surround his throne.
But servants of the heav'nly King May speak their joys a - broad.
We're marching thro' Im - man- uel's ground To fair - er worlds on high.

NO, NOT ONE!

REV. JOHNSON OATMAN, JR.

GEO. C. HUGG.

Slow, and with great feeling.

1. There's not a friend like the low - ly Je-sus, No, not one! no, not one!
2. No friend like Him is so high and ho-ly, No, not one! no, not one!
3. There's not an hour that He is not near us, No, not one! no, not one!
4. Did ev - er Saint find this friend forsake him? No, not one! no, not one!
5. Was e'er a gift like the Sav-iour giv-en? No, not one! no, not one!

None else could heal all our soul's dis-eas-es, No, not one! no, not one!
And yet no friend is so meek and low-ly, No, not one! no, not one!
No night so dark but His love can cheer us, No, not one! no, not one!
Or sin - ner find that He would not take him? No, not one! no, not one!
Will He re-fuse us a home in heav-en? No, not one! no, not one!

CHORUS.

Je - sus knows all a-bout our struggles, He will guide till the day is done,

There's not a friend like the low - ly Je-sus, No, not one! no, not one!

MAY MAURICE.   POWELL G. FITHIAN.

1. Sing the boundless love of Je - sus, One and all,   one and all ;
2. Sing the grace of Christ, our Sav- iour, One and all,   one and all ;
3. Sing, O sing a full sal - va - tion, One and all,   one and all ;
                              One and all,   one and all ;

How from sin and guilt he frees us, One and all,   one and all.
Sing his wondrous loving fa - vor, One and all,   one and all.
Tell it out to ev-'ry na - tion, One and all,   one and all.
                              One and all,   one and all.

CHORUS.

Till across the si - lent riv - er We shall hear the Master's call,

Let us chant his praises ev - er, One and all,   one and all.
                                          one and all.

One and all,

SOME DAY THE WALLS WILL FALL.

Rev. Johnson Oatman, Jr.

Geo. C. Hugg.

1. Soldiers of Christ, do not for-get That God is o - ver all;
2. Tho' you have la-bored with some friend To heed the Saviour's call,
3. Tho' walls of sin your way op-pose, Let not these things ap - pall;
4. Then all thro' life keep this in mind, That God is o - ver all;

And if by faith you trust him yet, Some day the walls will fall,.........
Your faith will triumph in the end; Some day the walls will fall,.........
You yet will con-quer all your foes, Some day the walls will fall,.........
So work and pray, and then by faith Some day the walls will fall,.........

CHORUS.

Some day the walls will fall. Then keep on marching ev'ry day, Un-til you

hear the call ;.... For if you labor as you pray, Some day the walls will fall.

MY FATHER'S HAND.

REV. JOHNSON OATMAN, JR.

GEO. C. HUGG.

1. I am on my way to a home on high, And I sing glad songs
2. Let the way be dark, let the way be light, Let the clouds ap - pear
3. I have rest, sweet rest, for my wea - ry feet, For my hun - gry soul,
4. I shall reach that land if I watch and pray, There are foes to fight

as the hours pass by, All the way thro' life toward that sum-mer land,
or the sun-shine bright, By the help of God, I shall reach that strand,
an-gel's food to eat, For all that I need my dear Lord has planned,
all a - long the way, But I fear not sa - tan, nor all his band,

CHORUS.

I am be - ing led by my Father's hand.
I am be - ing led by my Father's hand.
I am be - ing led by my Father's hand.
I am be - ing led by my Father's hand.

O my Father's hand, loving

Fa-ther's hand, Leads me on my way to the gold - en land; When I'm

weak and faint, I am made to stand, By the help I get from my Father's hand.

STEERING THAT WAY.

Rev. Johnson Oatman, Jr.

Geo. C. Hugg.

With feeling.

1. I've a man-sion all read-y   In that fair land of   day;
2. That fair man-sion in glo-ry   Time will nev-er de-cay;
3. Ma-ny loved ones are wait-ing   Till I've finished life's fray;
4. Tho' this life and its pleasures   Oft would bid me to stay,
5. There I'll see my dear Sav-iour,   If I trust and o-bey,

I   shall soon reach those por-tals,   Steer-ing   that   way.
I   shall soon see   its beau-ty,   Steer-ing   that   way.
Then   I'll meet them in heav-en,   Steer-ing   that   way.
Still   I   long for the king-dom,   Steer-ing   that   way.
Where   no night ev-er com-eth,   Steer-ing   that   way.

CHORUS.

Steering that way, (that way), Steering that way, Fair land o'er the o-cean,

I'm steer-ing that way;   Steer-ing that way, (that way), Steer-ing that

way,   Fair land o'er the o-cean, I'm steer-ing that way. (that way).

NOT WORTHY.

Sir Henry W. Baker.

Geo. C. Hugg.

1. I am not worth-y, Ho - ly Lord, That Thou shouldst come to me;
2. I am not worth-y, cold and bare, The lodg - ing of my soul;
3. I am not worth-y, yet my God, How can I say Thee nay;
4. O come! in the di - vin - est hour, Feed me with food di - vine;

Speak but the word, one gra - cious word Can set the sin - ner free.
How canst thou deign to en - ter there? Lord, speak, and make me whole.
Thee who didst give Thy flesh and blood, My ran - som price to pay.
And fill with all Thy love and pow'r, This worth-less heart of mine.

CHORUS.

I am not worthy, O no, not worthy That Thou shouldst come to me;

Speak but the word, one gra - cious word Can set the sin - ner free.

GATHERING IN THE GRAIN.

REV. JOHNSON OATMAN, JR.

GEO. C. HUGG.

Not too fast.

1. Gath - er - ing in the grain in the morn - ing sun;
2. Gath - er - ing in the grain that was sown in tears;
3. Gath - er - ing in the grain, tho' the storm - cloud rolls;
4. Gath - er - ing in the grain from the field so wide;
5. Gath - er - ing in the grain, while on earth we roam;

Gathering in the grain till the sheaves are won; Gathering in the
Gathering in the grain thro' the fleeting years; Gathering in the
Gathering in the grain that the Lord controls; Gathering in the
Gathering in the grain till the e - ven-tide; Gathering in the
Gathering in the grain till we cross the foam; Gathering in the

grain till the day is done; Gathering in the gold - en grain.
grain till the Lord ap - pears; Gathering in the gold - en grain.
grain of im - mor - tal souls; Gathering in the gold - en grain.
grain by the Sav - iour's side; Gathering in the gold - en grain.
grain for the har - vest home; Gathering in the gold - en grain.

CHORUS.

Gath - 'ring in the gold - en grain, Gath-
Yes, we're gather - ing Yes, we're

'ring in the gold - en grain; Gath - 'ring in the
gathering Yes, we're gathering

gold - en grain, Yes, we're gath - er - ing in the gold - en grain.

BADEA. S. M.

CHARLES WESLEY.　　　　　　　　　　　GERMAN MELODY.

1. A charge to keep I have, A God to glo - ri - fy,
2. To save the pres - ent age, My call - ing to ful - fill,
3. Arm me with jeal - ous care As in thy sight to live,
4. Help me to watch and pray And on thy - self re - ly,

A nev - er - dy - ing soul to save And fit it for the sky.
Oh, may it all my pow'rs engage To do my Master's will.
And O, thy ser - vant, Lord, prepare A strict ac - count to give.
As - sure, if I my trust be - tray, I shall for - ev - er die.

Ida L. Reed.

Powell G. Fithian.

1. Something to do for the Master each day, Let us find something to do;
2. Something to do for our Saviour and King, Let us find something to do;
3. Something to do, let us seek it to-day, Let us find something to do;

Serving him tru-ly will brighten the way, Let us find something to do.
Each lit-tle, loving deed blessing will bring, Let us find something to do.
Let us by loving deeds gladden the way, Let us find something to do.

Spreading the sunshine wher-ev-er we go, Glad to be helpful, tho'
We may the sor-row-ing comfort and cheer, Lead back the straying to
Je-sus will help us, our strength will sustain, If we will serve him with

lit-tle it be; We may find something for Je-sus to do, Joyful the
pathways of right; Some place is waiting for each of us here, Soon will the
willing hearts free; Blessings will follow, it can-not be vain, If ev-er

REFRAIN.

service to each one will be.) Some - - thing to do............. as the
daylight fade in - to the night. }
faithful to him we will be.) Something to do,   yes, something to do as the

days   go   by,........ Let............ us find some - - thing to
days go by, the days go by, Let us find something, yes, let us find something to

do ;.................... We....... may be help - - ful to him,.... if we
do, something to   do ; We may be helpful,   we may be helpful to him, to him, if we

try,....... Let...:...... us find some - - thing to do.......................
try, if we try, Let us find something, yes, let us find something to   do, something to   do.

REDEEMED.

"I have redeemed thee."—Isaiah 43: 1.

MAY MAURICE.   POWELL G. FITHIAN.

1. I lay bound and help - less in the toils of sin,
2. I will glad - ly fol - low where my Sav - iour leads,
3. Come, O come to Je - sus, why will you de - lay?

All was dark a - round me, all was dark with - in;
Through the tan - gled wildwood, or through flow - 'ry meads;
Now he waits to save you, why not come to - day?

Je - sus, full of pit - y, left his home a - bove, Came my soul to
By his love en - cir - cled, naught of ill I fear, Sing - ing as I
What a bless - ed Sav - iour! All who will may come; Take his of - fered

res - cue, what a - maz - ing love! Je - sus has redeemed me,
jour - ney, so that all may hear: Je - sus has redeemed me,
par - don, share his hap - py home. Je - sus has redeemed me,

this shall be my song; Je - sus has redeemed me, I to him be - long.

MAKE ROOM.

Geo. C. Hugg.   Geo. C. Hugg.

1. Make room for the Blessed Phy-si-cian, Who healeth the pal-sied and
2. Make room for the Blessed Phy-si-cian, Who healeth the sick and the
3. He com-fort-eth, healeth, and cheereth, He bringeth sal-va-tion this

lame, Who cast-eth out spir-its, and dev-ils, And rais-eth the
blind, Re-liev-ing dis-tress-es and sor-row, With pow-er, and
day, Come in-to our hearts, blessed Je-sus, Yea come, and a-

CHORUS.

dead from the grave.)
heal-ing di-vine. } He com-eth! He com-eth! Sal-va-tion pro-
bide Thou al-way.)

claim-ing, The Heal-er is pass-ing this way; He com-eth! He

cometh! The lost ones reclaiming, He com-eth! He com-eth! to-day.

STILL CLOSER.

BESSIE Q. JORDAN. POWELL G. FITHIAN.

1. I'm saved, O Lord, yes, praise thy name! I would with trumpet voice proclaim
2. Draw me so close that I may hear When thou wouldst whisper in my ear;
3. O glorious Sun, I'd gaze on thee, Till I no oth-er ob-ject see;
4. No oth-er pray'r my soul can learn, For thee a-lone my soul doth yearn;

The blessed news! But I would be Drawn dai-ly clos-er, Lord, to thee.
So close that thro' all earthly noise I clearly hear my Saviour's voice.
And yet would plead if 'tis thy will Draw me a lit-tle clos-er still.
My pray'r throughout e-ter-ni-ty, A lit-tle clos-er, Lord, to thee.

CHORUS.

Clos-er still,.......... yes, clos-er still, Ev-er
Clos-er still, yes, clos-er still,

clos-er, Lord, to thee, Bless-ed Sav-iour, I would be; And, ac-

cord - - ing to thy will, More like thee I fain would be.
And according thy blessed will,

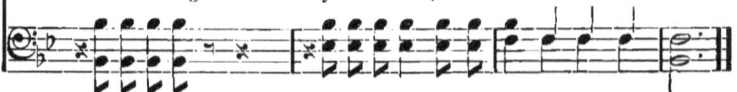

JESUS, SAVIOUR, WE ARE COMING.

IDA L. REED.   ADAM GEIBEL.

*DUETT.
Andante, with expression.

1. Je - sus, Sav - iour, we are com - ing, All Thy chil - dren far and near,
2. Make us pure   and ho - ly heart - ed, Worthy, Lord, Thine own to be,
3. All our lives,   O Lord, we give Thee, Wilt Thou take the gift we pray,

Gath'ring in   Thine earthly tem - ple, Wilt Thou bend our songs to hear.
We would march   beneath Thy ban - ner, Glad - ly   we would fol - low Thee.
Make us strong   a - gainst tempta - tion, Lead us   on   our upward way.

CHORUS.
We will praise   Striving all

We will praise Thy name for-ev - er,   Striving all Thy laws to keep,

Guide our steps

Guide our steps O bless-ed Sav - iour, Safe - ly up life's rugged steep.

*This piece may be sung with good effect as a Duett and Quartette.

"WASH ME, AND I SHALL BE WHITER THAN SNOW."

(VERY EFFECTIVE AS A SOLO.)

Rev. Johnson Oatman, Jr.   Powell G. Fithian.

1. I come to thee, Lord, all covered with sin, I come to be
2. Long, long I have wandered in this world so cold, But back to its
3. Whit- er than snowdrifts, O Lord, make my heart, Whiter than
4. Lord, make my heart pure, then I shall see thee, When from these sad

washed in Cal - va - ry's flow; O turn not a - way, dear
haunts, Lord, bid me not go; Tho' I am un - clean I'd
an - y - thing earth can show; Bid all the tra - ces
scenes I'll ver - y soon go; As pure as the lil - y, dear

Lord, take me in, "Now wash me, and I shall be whit- er than snow."
en - ter thy fold, "Now wash me, and I shall be whit- er than snow."
of sin de- part, "Now wash me, and I shall be whit- er than snow."
Lord, I would be, "Now wash me, and I shall be whit- er than snow."

CHORUS.

O Lord, wash me now, and cleanse me from sin, Just now, while I wait, let the crim-son tide flow: Lord, "Purge me with hys-sop and

I shall be clean, Now wash me, and I shall be whit-er than snow."

PLEYEL'S HYMN. 7.

IGNACE PLEYEL.

1. When this song of praise shall cease, Let thy children, Lord, de - part
2. O, where'er our path may lie, Father, let us not for - get
3. Blind are we, and weak and frail; Be thine aid for - ev - er near;

With the bless-ing of thy peace, And thy love in ev-'ry heart.
That we walk beneath thine eye, That thy care upholds us yet.
May the fear to sin pre - vail O - ver ev - 'ry oth - er fear.

CLOSE BY THE SIDE OF JESUS.

W. E. M.

Wm. Edie Marks.

1. There's a safe a - bid - ing place, Close by the side of Je - sus;
2. Ev - 'ry soul can rest se - cure, Close by the side of Je - sus;
3. More of heav'n we al - ways learn, Close by the side of Je - sus;
4. Sweet the moments, sweet the hours, Spent at the side of Je - sus;

'Tis for all of Is - rael's race, Close by the side of Je - sus.
All the storms of life en- dure, Close by the side of Je - sus.
Ho - ly fires with - in us burn, When by the side of Je - sus.
Bliss for - ev - er - more is ours, Close by the side of Je - sus.

CHORUS.

It is sweet to lin - ger there, Close by the side of Je - sus;

Free from sor - row, free from care, Close by the side of Je - sus.

THINE.

F. R. HAVERGAL.

GEO. C. HUGG.

1. Take my life and let it be, Con-se-cra-ted, Lord, to Thee;
2. Take my feet and let them be, Swift and beau-ti-ful for Thee;
3. Take my lips and let them be, Filled with mes-sa-ges for Thee;
4. Take my mo-ments and my days, Let them flow in end-less praise;
5. Take my will and make it Thine; It shall be no long-er mine;
6. Take my love, my Lord, I pour At Thy feet its treas-ure store!

Take my hands and let them move, At the im-pulse of Thy love.
Take my voice and let me sing, Al-ways, on-ly for my King.
Take my sil-ver and my gold,—Not a mite would I with-hold.
Take my in-te-lect, and use Ev-'ry pow'r as Thou shalt choose.
Take my heart it is Thine own,—It shall be Thy roy-al Throne.
Take my-self, and I will be, Ev-er, on-ly, all for Thee.

CHORUS.

All I am, or hope to be; Con-se-crate me Lord to Thee:

Seal me with Thy blood di-vine, Make me ev-er, on-ly Thine.

HEAVEN TO ME IS DEARER.

W. E. M.

WM. EDIE MARKS.

1. As moments fly,   as they go by,   Heaven to me   is near - er;
2. Father has gone, left me a- lone, Now he is rest - ing yon - der;
3. Yes, one by one, loved ones have gone, Leaving me sad and wea - ry;

Friends leave me here, they gather there, And heav'n to me   is dear - er.
Mother is there, beau - ti - ful, fair, Dressed in her robe of splen - dor.
With bonds so strong, it makes me long   To be with them in glo - ry.

CHORUS.

Tho' earthly ties   are sev- ered here,   It but makes heaven near - er;

Friends leave me here, they gather there ; Heaven to me   is dear - er.

AS THE DAYS GO BY.

REV. J. R. COLLIER, D.D.   H. S. LOWING.

1. Bless-ed Sav-iour un - to Thee,   Lo!   I come on bend-ed knee,
2. Count-less sins and faults I own,   Sins which I   can-not a - tone;
3. Ho - ly Je - sus, I would be   Ev - er-more conformed to Thee!
4. Make me ho - ly, dear-est Lord;   Feed   me on the bless-ed word;

All my fol - lies to con - fess,   And   to seek Thy right-eous-ness.
Care-less words and thoughts I mourn,   E - vil deeds in   sor - row borne.
Ev - 'ry thought and wish be Thine,   All Thy grac-es   in me shine!
Fill my soul with love to Thee,   Ev - er-more my help-er   be!

REFRAIN.

Je - sus, Sav-iour! hear my cry—And bless me, bless me, as the days go by!
O   my Sav-iour! hear my cry—And bless me, as the passing days go by!
O   my Sav-iour! hear my cry—And save me, save me as the days go by!
Bless-ed Sav-iour! hear my cry—And use me, use me as the days go by!

Je - sus, Sav-iour! hear my cry—And bless me, bless me as the days go by!
O   my Sav-iour! hear my cry—And bless me, as the passing days go by!
O   my Sav-iour! hear my cry—And save me, save me as the days go by!
Bless-ed Sav-iour! hear my cry—And use me, use me as the days go by!

WE SHALL HEAR HIM SAY, "WELL DONE."

W. E. M.

WM. EDIE MARKS.

1. O let us work with un - bat - ing zeal for Je - sus, Work till our
2. O let us work while the morn of life's up - on us, While in our
3. Up and be do - ing, for life is growing short- er, Life's e - ven-

earth - ly course is run ; Work till we're summoned to greater fields of
youthful strength and zeal ; Now is the time we can do the most for
tide comes on a - pace ; If we would hear Je - sus say the words of

CHORUS.

ser- vice, Then we shall hear him say, "Well done.")
Je - sus, Ere age has stamped us with his seal. } Soon will our earthly
welcome, We must be work- ing all our days.)

course be run, Soon we will see life's setting sun ; Af- ter we leave earthly

toil and go to heav - en, Je - sus will say to us, "Well done."

Mrs. Harriet E. Jones.

Geo. C. Hugg.

Trustingly.

1. Lift me high - er, blessed   Je - sus,   That for Thee   I firm - ly stand;
2. Lord, for- bid   that I should doubt Thee, O,   in-crease my faith, I   pray;
3. Lift me high - er, blessed   Je - sus,   On the heights, O   let me stand;

To the heights of grace, O   lift me,   Let me walk in Beu - lah-land.
I would trust in Thee, O   Sav-iour, More and more each hap - py day.
Lift me high - er bless-ed   Je - sus,   Let me gain the gold - en land.

CHORUS.

Lift   me high - er,   lift   me high-er,   High - er raise   my

p

. trust-ing soul; Bear me through the shin - ing por - tals, Let   the

f *Rallentando.*

pearl - y gates un - fold,   Let the pearl - y gates   un - fold.

W. E. M.

WM. EDIE MARKS.

1. Je - sus sat - is - fies, Je - sus sat - is - fies, All things now in him
2. When my hungry soul longs for bread divine, To my Saviour I
3. If I go athirst to the fount of love, And its quenching flood
4. O that men would learn to ex - alt the Lord; Je - sus sat - is - fies

I ob - tain; And my bless - ed Lord all my wants supplies;
al - ways go; He, on food sublime, feeds this soul of mine;
I de - sire, My Re - deem - er will all my thirst re - move
praise his name! O that all would praise him with one ac - cord;

CHORUS.

Je - sus sat - is - fies, bless his name!
Je - sus sat - is - fies, this I know.
And with bliss di - vine me in - spire.
Je - sus sat - is - fies, praise his name!

Je - sus sat - is - fies,

Je - sus sat - is - fies, Je - sus sat - is - fies, bless his name! All in

him I gain, each de - sire ob - tain; Je - sus sat - is - fies, bless his name!

THE BIBLE IS MY GUIDE.

THE BIBLE IS MY GUIDE.

Rev. Johnson Oatman, Jr.　　　　　　　Adam Geibel.

1. I am a pil-grim to a land, That's on the oth-er side;
2. The mar-in-er who steers by thee, Will all the storms out-ride;
3. How ma-ny points in life I find, That I can-not de-cide;
4. And when I reach at close of day, The Jor-don's i-cy tide;

But I shall safe-ly reach that strand, The Bi-ble is my guide.
So while I cross life's roll-ing sea, The Bi-ble is my guide.
I dare not trust in my own mind, The Bi-ble is my guide.
I'll sim-ply close my eyes and say, The Bi-ble is my guide.

CHORUS.

O bless-ed Word of God most high, I'll in Thy truths a-bide;

In all my path-way to the sky, The Bi-ble is my guide.

WHAT HAS JESUS DONE FOR ME?

W. E. M.

WM. EDIE MARKS.

1.   O, what has Je-sus done for me? He has tak-en all my sins a-way;
2. What more has Je-sus done for me? He has cleansed me with his blood, I know;
3. What more has Je-sus done for me? He has taught my lips to sing and pray;
4. What more has Je-sus done for me? He has giv-en me a hap-py song;

What more has Je-sus done for me? He has turned me from my downward way.
What more has Je-sus done for me? He has washed me just as white as snow.
What more has Je-sus done for me? He has blest me all a-long the way.
What more has Je-sus done for me? He has set me singing all day long.

Chorus.

And I shall sing his praises here, Till I breathe up-on the earth my last;

Then I shall praise him o-ver there, When the pilgrimage of life is past.

"O SAVIOUR DEAR, SPEAK WORDS OF CHEER."

Rev. Johnson Oatman, Jr.   Adam Geibel.

1. A storm one time was rag - ing wild, Up - on the might-y deep;
2. But fear - ful cries disturbed His sleep, And made His bo-som thrill;
3. When we a - mid the storms of life, Can sink in - to His will;
4. When sor-rows come, and tri - als sweep, The Sav - iour knows it all;
5. He watch-es o'er us night and day, Tho' we may be a - sleep;

But calm - ly as a lit - tle child, Our Sav - iour lay a - sleep.
Then He a - rose, re - buked the deep, And all around was still.
We hear His voice a - bove the strife, Still say - ing, "peace be still."
No more a - sleep up - on the deep, He hears the faint-est call.
And He will guide us if we pray, A - cross life's storm-y deep.

CHORUS.

O Sav - iour dear, speak words of cheer, When we are tempest tossed;

We will not fear, , if Thou art near, With-out Thee we are lost.

LET MY CLEANSING BE COMPLETE.

E. A. H.

REV. ELISHA A. HOFFMAN.

1. Bending, Lord, be- fore thee low - ly, Let my cleansing be complete;
2. All my na- ture needs re - fin - ing, Let my cleansing be complete;
3. Sanc-ti - fy my soul- af - fections, Let my cleansing be complete;
4. I am thirsting for the blessing, Let my cleansing be complete;
5. Self and sin I come be - moaning, Let my cleansing be complete;
6. To be thine thy love inspired me, Let my cleansing be complete:

Pur - i - fy and make me ho - ly, Let my cleansing be complete.
Needs with-in thine im - age shining, Let my cleansing be complete.
Lord, re-move my im - per-fections, Let my cleansing be complete.
My un - ho - li - ness con - fess- ing, Let my cleansing be complete.
Wash me in the blood a - ton-ing, Let my cleansing be complete.
Nev - er have I so de-sired thee, Let my cleansing be complete.

CHORUS.

Let my cleansing be com-plete; Here the blessing I en-treat;
complete; entreat;

Sanc-ti- fy me wholly, make me pure and low-ly, Let my cleansing be complete.
complete.

W. S.

WM. STONE.

1. I'm bound for the heav'nly kingdom, My treas-ure is set on high;
2. I'm bound for the heav'nly kingdom, Where there's not a tear nor sigh;
3. I'm bound for the heav'nly kingdom, I've lov'd ones beyond the sky;
4. I'm bound for the heav'nly kingdom, O sin-ner why don't you try;

With Je - sus I'll live in glo-ry, Yes, that is the rea - son why.
My Fa-ther in heav'n has told me, Yes, that is the rea - son why.
Some day I shall go to meet them, Yes, that is the rea - son why.
For a home of e-ternal glo-ry, Yes, that is the rea - son why.

CHORUS.

Glo - ry, glo-ry, hal - le - lu - jah! I'm bound for the

heav'n-ly king-dom, And Je - sus will wel - come me there.

"COME, FOLLOW ME."

W. E. M.

WM. EDIE MARKS.

1. One day I heard the Sav - iour say, "Come, fol - low me;
2. His sweet voice charmed my soul and heart, "Come, fol - low me;"
3. I could no long - er hes - i - tate, When called by him;
4. He bade me then take up the cross And fol - low him;

Leave all be - hind thee, right a - way, My child to be."
From him I can - not stay a - part; I'll fol - low thee.
I left be - hind my sin's es - tate, A crown to win.
All else I count - ed but as dross, He took my sin.

CHORUS.

"O wan - der - er," he called to me, "Come, fol - low me;"

His voice was sweetest mel - o - dy, "Come, fol - low me."

THE BLOOD UPON THE DOOR.

Rev. Johnson Oatman, Jr.

Geo. C. Hugg.

Slow, and with great expression.

1. When the Lord pass'd over E-gypt, There was weeping ev-'ry-where, For the
2. We are in a land of danger, And death lurks on ev-'ry hand, But that
3. Not the blood of lambs or cat-tle, Sprinkled o - ver an - y part, But the

an-gel smote the first-born, Of each family dwelling there, But some hous-es
soul has per-fect safe-ty, Who obeys the Lord's command, For se - cure in
blood of Christ the Saviour, Can redeem a hu-man heart, Then when death these

he pass'd o - ver, As his word had said be-fore, And death entered not the
God's pa-vil- ion, He can watch life's breakers roar, For God's angels guard that
ties shall sev-er, And we walk on earth no more, We may live with Christ for -

CHORUS.

por-tals, Where the blood was on the door.
dwelling, Where the blood is on the door. } Pre-cious blood up - on the door, Sav-ing
ev- er, If *His* blood is on the door.

blood up-on the door, O my soul there is no danger, When the blood is on the door.

E. A. H. REV. ELISHA A. HOFFMAN.

1. My life flows a - long in gladness and song, Since Je - sus re-
2. No heart can conceive the life I now live, Since Je - sus re-
3. My faith is made sure, my hope is se - cure, Since Je - sus re-
4. As on- ward I go the pathway be - low, Since Je - sus re-

newed my soul; My heart and my tongue his goodness prolong,
newed my soul; What peace he can give, what joys I re - ceive,
newed my soul; His love keeps me pure and helps me en - dure,
newed my soul, He grace doth be- stow, he lov - eth me so,

CHORUS.

Since I was made conscious- ly whole. What measures of peace and of

bless - ing Each moment en - rapture my soul; What wonderful

streams of re - fresh - ing, Since I was made conscious - ly whole!

E. E. HEWITT.   ADAM GEIBEL.

1. Not a moun-tain streamlet, Singing as it flows, But the way be-
2. Not a lit - tle spar - row Flut-ters to the ground, Not a hun - gry
3. Not a con - trite spir - it, Seek-ing for re - lief Comes in faith to

fore it, God our Father knows. Not a star that circles In the midnight
rob - in In the for-est found, But our Fa-ther se - eth, Car-eth for their
Je - sus, With its load of grief, But His voice so ten-der, Whispers peace with-

sky, But is 'neath the guid - ing Of His watchful eye.
need, Not a cry of sor - row, But His ear takes heed.
in, And His blood, so pre - cious, Cleanseth from all sin.

CHORUS.

Not a life too low - ly, For the Fa - ther's care,

Not a heart too lone - ly, In His love to share.

TRYING TO BE MORE LIKE JESUS.

W. E. M.

WM. EDIE MARKS.

1. I am try-ing the best I can To be more and more like Je-sus;
2. I am striving to be like him, Trying to be more like Je-sus;
3. That ex-am-ple he gave to me, I will cop-y in his ser-vice;
4. As I walk in the path he went, As I try to be like Je-sus;

Im-i-ta-ting the Son of Man, Trying to be more like Je-sus.
Ev-er wishing to be with-in Just a lit-tle more like Je-sus.
This my mot-to in life shall be: "Trying to be more like Je-sus.
This the prayer dai-ly upward sent: "On-ly to be more like Je-sus.

CHORUS.

Ev-er try-ing the best I know To be more and more like Je-sus;

Ev-er striving like him to go; Trying to be more like Je-sus.

JESUS NEVER LEAVES THE SHIP.

Suggested by the sinking of the steamship Elbe, in the North Sea, Jan. 30th, 1895, in which over 300 lives were lost, and brave Captain Von Goessel *went down with his ship.*

REV. JOHNSON OATMAN, JR.   GEO. C. HUGG.

1. When up-on life's roll-ing o - cean, Fraught with danger is the trip;
2. When the waves are dashing o'er her, Do not fear tho' she may dip;
3. O look up, why are ye fear - ful? Why look down with trembling lip?
4. Oft the ves-sel we must light-en, From all worldly things must strip;
5. Sin - ner come and sail for Heav-en, Have no fears a-bout the trip;

Do not fear 'mid the com-mo - tion,   Je - sus nev - er leaves the ship.
Bet - ter skies yet lie be - fore her,   Je - sus nev - er leaves the ship.
Dry your eyes now sad and tear - ful,   Je - sus nev - er leaves the ship.
Then we'll find as the skies brighten,   Je - sus nev - er leaves the ship.
All on board to Him are giv - en,   Je - sus nev - er leaves the ship.

CHORUS.

Put your trust in your com-man - der,   Not a foot on board shall slip;

In yon port He'll safely land her,   Je - sus nev - er leaves the ship.

TILL HE COMETH.

W. E. M.

Wm. Edie Marks.

1. To my Lord I will be true, Till he com - eth, In what
2. If sup- port - ed by his pow'r Till he com - eth, I will
3. Un - til Je - sus comes to reign, Till he com - eth, To the

ev - er I may do, Till he com - eth; If the
la - bor hour by hour, Till he com - eth, I will
world I will proclaim, Till he com - eth; All the

Lord may ev - er call Me to tasks both great and small, I will
do my best for him, And will strive the world to win From en-
rich - es of his grace, And his name I'll ev - er praise, While I

CHORUS.

glad - ly do them all, Till he com - eth. Till he com - eth
tic - ing snares of sin, Till he com - eth. We will work and sing and pray,
wait for ma - ny days, Till he com - eth.

Till he com - eth, I will work and sing and pray

I will work and sing and pray,

Till he com - eth; I will la - bor ev - 'ry day, And my

Lord I will o- bey, While I watch and sing and pray, Till he com - eth.

O LORD, RENEW THY WORK.

WILLIAM HUGHES.   V. PAUL JONES.

1. O Lord, re - new thy work; Send down thy quick'ning pow'r,
2. O let me know thy love With - in my heart doth live:
3. O Lord, as here I kneel, Thy pard'ning grace be - stow;

And let me feel thy presence near, This ver - y hour.
To thee, my life, my - self, my all, I free - ly give.
Wash me with thine all - cleansing blood As white as snow.

E. A. H.　　　　　　　　　　　　Rev. Elisha A. Hoffman.

1. I have peace with - in my soul, hal - le - lu - jah!
2. I have found in him a Friend, hal - le - lu - jah!
3. Mine, the bles - sed Mer - cy Seat, hal - le - lu - jah!
4. O the pros - pect on be - fore, hal - le - lu - jah!

Je - sus' blood has made me whole, hal - le - lu - jah!
Whose sweet friendship will not end, hal - le - lu - jah!
Mine, com - mun - ion rich and sweet, hal - le - lu - jah!
O the home on heav - en's shore, hal - le - lu - jah!

He has ban - ished self and sin, Reigns up - on the throne with-
If I go to him in prayer, Seek his ten - der lov - ing
Fel - low - ship and peace di - vine, Wealth of love and joy are
O the robe, and palm, and crown, When the cross I shall lay

D.S.—theme of song shall be, Praise to him who so loves

Fine.

in Keeps the tem - ple pure and clean, hal - le - lu - jah!
care, His kind fa - vor I shall share, hal - le - lu - jah!
mine, Since I all to him re - sign, hal - le - lu - jah!
down, In yon cit - y of re - nown, hal - le - lu - jah!

me, Whom in heav'n I hope to see, hal - le - lu - jah!

CHORUS.

Hal - le - lu - jah! Hal - le - lu - jah! Hal - le-
Hal - le - lu - jah! Hal- le - lu - jah!

D.S.

lu - jah for - ev - er and for - ev - er! This my
for - ev - er, hal- le - lu - jah!

O WHAT WONDROUS LOVE!

WILLIAM HUGHES.   V. PAUL JONES.

1. I am hap- py in the love of Je - sus, Coming from the throne a- bove,
2. Je- sus knows my ev-'ry sin and weakness, He will keep me all the day;
3. He is always near to shield and com- fort When temptations dark be- tide;

For it fills my soul with joy and glad - ness: O what wondrous love!
He, my comfort, by the hand doth take me, Leads me all the way.
When the way is rough, the road is wea - ry, He is at my side.

I EXPECT TO WIN THE PRIZE BY AND BY.

Rev. Johnson Oatman, Jr.   Adam Geibel.

1. I am on the race course run - ning t'ward the goal, Where a
2. All the world is look - ing on from day to day, Clouds of
3. Toys of earth are try - ing to al - lure me back, But I
4. Earth no more can charm me with its cares and strife, With God's

glit - t'ring prize has caught my eye; With the help of Je - sus
wit - ness - es are press - ing nigh; But tho' sin and Sa - tan
keep my eyes turn'd t'ward the sky; Nev - er can the temp-ter
help I'll run un - til I die; Then my Lord has prom-ised

who redeem'd my soul, I ex - pect to win the prize by and by.
try to block my way, I ex - pect to win the prize by and by.
throw me off the track, I ex - pect to win the prize by and by.
me a crown of life, I ex - pect to win the prize by and by.

CHORUS.

I ex - pect to win, yes, I ex - cept to win, See a

bright, bright crown is held on high, "Look-ing un - to Je - sus

with-out weight or sin, I ex - pect to win the prize by and by.

VIGIL.

THOS. KELLEY.

PEISELLO.

1. A - rise, my saints, a - rise!   The Lord, our lead - er is:
2. We soon shall see the day   When all our toils shall cease;
3. This hope sup-ports us here;   It makes our bur-dens light;
4. Till, of the prize pos - sessed,   We hear of war no more;

The foe be-fore His ban-ner flies, And vic - to - ry is His.
When we shall cast our arms a-way, And dwell in end - less peace.
'T will serve our droop-ing hearts to cheer, Till faith shall end in sight:
And ev - er with our Lead-er rest, On yon-der peace-ful shore.

HASTE TO THE CROSS.

120

Edgar Page.

James McGranahan.

1. Come, hast-en, poor, wea-ry one, haste to the cross, For Je-sus is
2. No mat-ter how heav-y the bur-den may be, Nor how thou art
3. Tho' Sa-tan may tell thee that thou art too base To mer-it the
4. "Ye burdened and wea-ry ones, come un-to me, And I will give

calling to - day; Wait not to be bet-ter, nor suf-fer a loss
pressed by the load; The bur-den will light-en and vanish a-way,
Saviour's kind care, De-spair not; wher-ev-er thou seekest his face
un-to you rest;" So call-ed the Saviour, and calleth to thee

CHORUS.

By tar-ry-ing yet by the way.
While trav'ling the Cal-va-ry road.
He sure-ly will meet with thee there.
To come un-to him and be blest.

O haste to the cross, O
haste to the cross, The Saviour is waiting for thee!............ Is
is waiting for thee!

waiting to bless, is waiting to save; O come while he waiteth for thee!

Used by per. of E. A. Hoffman, owner of Copyright.

TAKE YOUR CROSS AND FOLLOW JESUS.

IDA L. REED.　　　　　　　　　　　　GEO. C. HUGG.

1. Take your cross and fol-low Je - sus, Bear it brave - ly as you go;
2. Take your cross and fol-low Je - sus, Faint not if the days be drear;
3. Take your cross and fol-low Je - sus, He will give you grace to bear;

This sweet tho't your soul will strengthen, All your tri - als He doth know.
Cling to His dear hand the clos-er, 'Till the shad-ows dis - ap - pear.
All the ills that vex and grieve you, If you seek His help in pray'r.

CHORUS.

Take your cross and fol - low Je - sus, He will help you day by day;

Ev - 'ry bur - den light-er seemeth, When to Him you trust the way.

WHEN I FIRST ASKED FOR PARDON.

W. E. M.

WM. EDIE MARKS.

1. My Saviour heard my plaintive pray'r When I first asked for par - don;
2. He was not slow to heed my call, When I first asked for par - don;
3. Goodness has followed me each day, Since I first asked for par - don;
4. O hap-py time! O hap-py day! When I first asked for par - don;

He freed me from the sins I bare, When I first asked for par - don.
In mer-cy he for-gave me all, When I first asked for par - don.
And mercy's found a - long the way, Since I first asked for par - don.
When Je - sus took my sins a - way, When I first asked for par - don.

CHORUS.

For - giveness Je - sus free - ly gave, When I first asked for par - don;

No dread of for - mer guilt I have, Since I first asked for par - don.

I KNOW THAT JESUS KEEPS.

Rev. W. J. Stuart, A. M.   Geo. C. Hugo.

1. A - mid the storm that sweeps,   Like bil - lows o'er the   soul;
2. I will not fear the   deeps   Of dark-ness nor of   pain;
3. There's for the eye that   weeps,   A   rest both sure and   sweet;
4. The death that on-ward creeps,   Has lost its sting for   me;
5. And when I've climb'd the steeps   Of heav - en's bright do - main;

I know that Je - sus keeps,   That He has full con - trol.
I know that Je - sus keeps,   I shall see light a - gain.
I know that Je - sus keeps,   I've found a safe re - treat.
I know that Je - sus keeps,   His face at last I'll see.
I'll sing that Je - sus keeps,   With all the spot - less train.

Chorus.

He keeps, He keeps, I know He does, He holds me by His pow'r;

He keeps, He saves, I know He does, He's with me ev - 'ry hour.

E. A. H.   Rev. Elisha A. Hoffman.

1. Have thy affections been nailed to the cross? Is thy heart right with God?
2. Hast thou domin- ion o'er self and o'er sin? Is thy heart right with God?
3.   Is there no more condem- nation for sin? Is thy heart right with God?
4.   Are all thy pow'rs under Je - sus' control? Is thy heart right with God?
5.   Art thou now walking in heaven's pure light? Is thy heart right with God?

Dost thou count all things for Je- sus but loss? Is thy heart right with God?
O- ver all   e - vil without and with- in? Is thy heart right with God?
Does Je- sus rule in the   temple with- in? Is thy heart right with God?
Does he each moment a - bide in thy soul? Is thy heart right with God?
Is   thy soul wearing the garment of white? Is thy heart right with God?

CHORUS.

Is   thy heart right with   God, Washed in   the crim - son   flood,

Cleansed and made ho-ly, humble and low-ly, Right in the sight of   God?....
                                                                 of God?

THE LOVING NAME—JESUS.

WM. R. WINTERS.

GEO. C. HUGG.

With great feeling.

1. It fell up - on a sin - ner's ear, That sweetest name—Je - sus!
2. 'Twas wispered to a wea - ried heart, That cheering name—Je - sus!
3. It brought the wanderer back to God, That ten - der name—Je - sus!
4. 'Tis dear - er far than fame or wealth, That lov-liest name—Je - sus!

It ban-ished all His doubts and fears, That mightest name—Je - sus!
It bade all gloom and care de - part, That bless-ed name—Je - sus!
It guid - eth to you blest a - bode; That precious name—Je - sus!
'Twill res - cue from e - ter - nal death, That sav-ing name—Je - sus!

CHORUS.

Then sound it out on hill and plain, That wondrous name—Je - sus!

Ech. - o it o'er and o'er a - gain, That glo-rious name—Je - sus!

THERE'S ONLY ONE.

N.

JAMES McGRANAHAN.

1. There's on - ly One whose pit - y falls like dew up - on the wounded heart;
2. There's on - ly One who is not harsh, But ten - derness it- self to all;
3. There's on - ly One who can support, And who suf- ficient grace can give
4. O blessed Jesus, Friend of friends, Come, hide us 'neath thy shelt'ring arm;
5. Thou art the One, the on - ly One For whom no love too warm can flow;

There's on - ly One who nev - er stirs, Tho' en - e- my and friend depart.
There's on - ly One who knows each heart, And list- ens to its faintest call.
To bear up un - der ev- 'ry grief, And spotless in this world to live.
Come down a - mid this wicked world, And keep us from its guilt and harm.
Thou art the One, the on - ly one Who giv - est perfect rest be- low.

CHORUS.

There's on - ly One, there's on - ly One Can make us ev - er tru - ly blest;

There's on - ly One, there's on - ly One Can give us peace and perfect rest.

THE CITY OF LIGHT.

A. S. K.

A. S. KIEFFER.

1. { There's a cit - y of light 'mid the stars, we are told, Where they know not a
   { And the gates are of pearl, and the streets are of gold, And the build-ing ex -

2. { Brother dear, nev - er fear, we shall tri-umph at last, If we trust in the
   { When our tri-als and toils, and our weepings are past, We shall meet in that

CHORUS.

sor - row or care; }
ceed-ing-ly fair. } Let us pray for each oth - er, nor faint by the way,
word He has giv'n; }
home up in heav'n. }

In this sad world of sor - row and care, For that home is so

bright, and is al-most in sight, And I trust in my heart you'll go there.

3. Sister dear, never fear,—for the Saviour is near,
   With His hand He will lead you along;
   And the way that is dark Christ will graciously clear,
   And your mourning shall turn to a song.

4. Let us walk in the light of the gospel divine;
   Let us ever keep near to the cross;
   Let us love, watch, and pray, in our pilgrimage here;
   Let us count all things else but as loss.

E. A. H.   Rev. Elisha A. Hoffman.

1. Wondrous it seemeth to me,   Je - sus so gracious should be,
2. Heart of mine nev - er could know   Je - sus such peace could be - stow,
3. Once I was full of all sin,   Now, thro' the blood, I am clean;
4. Long I re - sist - ed his grace,   In my heart gave him no place,
5. He doth my new heart con - trol,   Cleansing and keeping me whole,

Mer - cy re - veal - ing, comforting, healing, Blessing a sinner like me.
Till the dear Saviour showed me his fa - vor, Cleansed my heart whiter than snow.
Willing to save me, pardon he gave me, And I am happy with - in.
But Jesus sought me till he had brought me, Penitent, seeking his face.
Ban - ish-ing sad - ness, with joy and gladness Filling and thrilling my soul.

CHORUS.

Is it not won - der- ful, is it not won - der- ful Je - sus so
Yes, it is won - der- ful, strange and so won - der- ful (*Omit.*)

gracious should be?............ :|| That he should save e - ven me!............
lov- ing and gracious should be? :|| That he should pardon and save even me!

JUST THE SAME.

F. R. HAVERGAL.

GEO. C. HUGG.

1. Thro' the yes - ter - day of a - ges, Je - sus, Thou hast been the same;
2. Joy - ful - ly we stand and wit - ness, Thou art still to - day the same;
3. Gaz - ing down the great for - ev - er, Bright - er glows the one sweet Name,

Thro' our own life's chequered pa - ges, Still the one dear changeless name,
In Thy per - fect, glo - rious fit - ness, Meet-ing ev' - ry need and claim,
Stead-fast ra-diance, pal - ing nev - er, Je - sus, Je - sus! still the same,

Well may we in Thee con - fide, Faith-ful Sav - iour, proved and tried.
Chief- est of ten thous-and, Thou ! Sav - iour, O, most pre - cious now !
Ev - er-more Thou shalt en - dure, Our own Sav - iour, strong and sure.

CHORUS.

Just the same Je - sus! The ver - y same Je - sus!

Thro' the cease-less, roll - ing a - ges, Je - sus, Thou art still the same.

W. E. M.
                                WM. EDIE MARKS.

1. O - ver- burdened with a weight of woe, Un - to my Re - deemer
2. Sin had compassed me with chains a - round, By its fet - ters I had
3. Ma - ny measures of re - lief I tried, But I nev - er could be

I did go; Now an ev - er - last - ing joy I know,
long been bound, But im - me - di - ate re - lief I found
sat - is - fied Un - til I had found the Cru - ci - fied,

CHORUS.

Je - sus took the bur - den off. } Je - - sus took the
When the Sav - iour took them off. } Je - - sus took the
Till he took the bur - den off. } Je - sus, Je - sus

bur - den off, Je - - sus took the bur - den off; I for
Je - sus, Je - sus

ev - er-more shall hap - py be, Je - sus took the bur - den off.

HE HAS COME.

HORATIUS BONAR.

ADAM GEIBEL.

1. He has come! the Christ of God; Left for us His glad a - bode;
2. He the might - y King has come! Making this poor earth His home,
3. Un - to us a child is born! Ne'er has earth be-held a morn

Stoop - ing from His throne of bliss; To this dark-some wil-der - ness.
Come to bear our sin's sad load; Son of Da - vid, Son of God.
All a - mong the morns of time. Half so glo - rious in its prime.

He, has come! the Prince of peace; Come to bid our sor - rows cease:
He has come, whose name of grace Speaks deliv'rance to our race;
Un - to us a Son is giv'n! He has come from God's own heav'n;

Come to scat - ter, with his light, All the shadows of our night.
Left for us His glad a - bode; Son of Man, and Son of God.
Bring-ing with Him from a - bove, Ho - ly peace and Ho - ly love.

"THE GOOD CAN NEVER DIE."

TO THE MEMORY OF PROF. JNO. R. SWENEY.

Written from fragments of thought thrown out at his funeral, on April 13th, 1899, by Ira D. Sankey, John Wanamaker, Dr. P. H. Mowry, Dr. Weston, Rev. E. A. Ballard, and others.

Rev. Johnson Oatman, Jr.   Geo. C. Hugg.

1. Tho' friends may gather round thee, their last respects to pay,
2. Thy life, thy work, dear broth - er, to all mankind be - longs,
3. "Ten thousand hearts are heav - y that are not here to - day,"
4. One more farewell, our broth - er, and yet 'twill not be long

It is a scene be - fit - ting thy "Cor - o - na - tion Day;"
"Be-'cause the world is bet - ter and brighter for thy songs;"
"Ten thousand eyes are weep - ing in cit - ies far a - way;"
Till we shall join in sing - ing with thee "The New, New Song."

For thee, our no - ble broth - er, "The sing - ing time has come,"
"A Fol - low - er of Je - sus," thy "thoughts were all a - bove;"
Thy spir - it now is hap - py with - in its "Beu - lah Land,"
"May we, like thee, be faith - ful un - til our work is done,"

For with the "an - gel con - voy" thy spir - it hath gone home.
Thy "soul was filled with mu - sic, thy heart was filled with love."
Thy "Ship has Crossed the O - cean," and reached the gold - en strand.
"Un - til our course is fin - ished, our crown of vic - t'ry won."

Copyright, 1899, by Geo. C. Hugg.

CHORUS.

Farewell, farewell, dear broth - er, un - til we grasp thy hand

And hear thee lead the sing - ing in yon - der glo - ry land;

"No time for tears of sor - row," for, tho' we say "Good-bye,"

Yet thou wilt live for - ev - er, "The good can nev - er die;"

Yet thou wilt live for - ev - er, "The good can nev - er die."

134 WITH JESUS.

This tune was written at Landisville Camp Meeting, season 1898, and is the last song by the lamented Sweney.

Rev. D. W. Gordon. Jno. R. Sweney.

1. When from the scenes of earth we rise, To find our home beyond the skies,
2. The storms of life will all be o'er, Our souls be tempest-tossed no more,
3. Redeemed from sin and saved by grace, We shall behold his blessed face,
4. With him in glo - ry e'er to stay, Where founts of liv - ing waters play,

What visions then shall greet our eyes, When we shall be with Je - sus !
When we have reach'd the golden shore, For we shall be with Je - sus.
The wonders of his love to trace, As we shall be with Je - sus.
And sorrow's tears are wiped a - way, For- ev - er - more with Je - sus.

CHORUS.

To be with Je - sus, O how sweet ! With saints and an - gels at his feet,

With songs we shall each oth- er greet, And ev - er be with Je - sus.

Of all the late Prof. Sweney's compositions, this is possibly the most widely known. It was sung at his funeral by Ira D. Sankey with joyfulness as a "Coronation Hymn" rather than a funeral dirge. Mr. Sankey voiced the true sentiment, when he said, "My brother is not dead, he has only moved from this beautiful world to a more glorious heritage."

E. P. STITES.   JNO. R. SWENEY.

1. I've reached the land of corn and wine, And all its rich-es free-ly mine;
2. The Saviour comes and walks with me, And sweet communion here have we;
3. A sweet perfume up-on the breeze Is borne from ev-er ver-nal trees,
4. The zephyrs seem to float to me, Sweet sounds of heaven's mel-o-dy,

Here shines undimm'd one blissful day, For all my night has pass'd a-way.
He gen-tly leads me with his hand, For this is heaven's borderland.
And flow'rs that nev-er fad-ing grow Where streams of life for-ev-er flow.
As an-gels, with the white-robed throng, Join in the sweet re-demption song.

CHORUS.

O Beulah land, sweet Beulah land, As on thy highest mount I stand,

I look a-way a-cross the sea, Where mansions are prepared for me,

And view the shining glo-ry shore, My heav'n, my home for-ev-er-more.

From "Goodly Pearls," by per. of John J. Hood.

FATHER HOLDS THE HAND.

TO BABY EVANGELINE HUGG.

These words were written by request, and lovingly inscribed to my little daughter, Evangeline, who, since she was two months old, would in the hours of midnight darkness place her little hand in her father's, and sweetly coo herself to sleep. God grant that we may "Enter the kingdom of heaven like a little child."

REV. JOHNSON OATMAN, JR.　　　　　　　　　GEO. C. HUGG.

DUET.

1. When darkness o - ver all the earth its sa - ble wing has spread,
2. Up - on the Christian's pathway here, how ma - ny trials are met,
3. Tho' thro' the val - ley we may tread, or o'er the mountain height,

The lit - tle babe is safe - ly tucked with - in its snow - y bed;
How oft - en long be - fore its time the sun has seemed to set;
Our bless - ed Lord will lead us thro' the darkness and the light;

And tho' the change from light to dark it can - not un - derstand,
But up - ward thro' the night and gloom Faith points her mystic wand,
And when up - on the Jordan's brink at last our feet shall stand,

The lit - tle one sinks off to sleep while fa - ther holds its hand.
And Hope hangs out her bea - con light, for Fa - ther holds the hand.
We will not fear to cross the tide, if Fa - ther holds the hand.

CHORUS.

Lord, give us faith to trust thee, tho' we may not un - derstand,

May we like lit - tle children rest, while Fa- ther holds the hand;

While Fa - ther holds the hand, while Fa - ther holds the hand,

May we like lit - tle children rest, while Fa- ther holds the hand.

WORK FOR JESUS EVERYWHERE.

E. E. HEWITT.   ADAM GEIBEL.

With spirit.

1. Work for Je - sus in your home - life, Kind - ly words and
2. Work for Je - sus, bless - ed Sav - iour, Pure and faith - ful
3. Work for Je - sus, no - ble la - bor! Sweet - er, earth can

win - ning way   Help to make the fire - side hap - py,
ev - er be,   Look - ing to the per - fect pat - tern,
nev - er know,   And the more we try His ser - vice,

Female voices only.

Help to speak your Sav - iour's praise ;   In your dai - ly
Let the world his beau - ty see ;   Work for Je - sus
Dear - er to our hearts 'twill grow ;   Work with Je - sus,

walk and bear - ing, Show the in - ner life Di - vine,
by the way - side, You will be the bet - ter heard,
Oh, how pre - cious ! Christ is watch - ing, work - ing too,

FULL CHORUS.

For the sake of those who love you, Let your light for
If your life is al - ways speaking, Then what pow'r goes
When He calls you up to Glo - ry, He will have a

CHORUS.

Je - sus shine.
with a word. } On the Sab - bath, on the week - day,
crown for you. }

As the mo - ments fly a - long, Work for Je - sus,

He's re - deemed you, Work with faith, and pray'r and song.

RISE, SOUL, AND CONFESS HIM.

E. A. H.　　　　　　　　　　　　　　　Rev. Elisha A. Hoffman.

1. Is Christ a Saviour from all sin? Con- fess him to the world;
2. Has Je - sus made all sin to cease? Con- fess him to the world;
3. For vic - t'ry in temp - ta- tion's hour, Con- fess him to the world;
4. Be- cause the Lord has so loved thee, Con- fess him to the world;
5. With grat - i- tude, in fer - vent love, Con- fess him to the world;

Thy heart, has Je - sus made it clean? Con- fess him to the world.
Has he bestowed his per- fect peace? Con- fess him to the world.
For faith and o - ver- com - ing pow'r, Con- fess him to the world.
Be- cause his grace has been so free, Con- fess him to the world.
Your loy - al - ty to Je - sus prove, Con- fess him to the world.

CHORUS.

Rise, soul, and con- fess him, And tell what he has done for thy soul;

Now faithful- ly wit - ness That Je- sus' blood hath made thee whole.

WALK IN THE LIGHT.

BERNARD BARTON.

GEO. C. HUGG.

1. Walk in the light! so shalt thou know That fel-low-ship of love, His
2. Walk in the light! and thou shalt find Thy heart made tru-ly His, Who
3. Walk in the light! and e'en the tomb No fear-ful shade shall wear; Glo-
4. Walk in the light! thy path shall be Peace-ful, se-rene, and bright; For

spir-it on-ly can be-stow, Who reigns in light a-bove.
dwells in cloud-less light en-shrined, In whom no dark-ness is.
ry shall chase a-way its gloom, For Christ has con-quered there.
God by grace, shall dwell in thee, And God him-self is light.

CHORUS.

Walk............ in the light!................. Walk............ in the
Walk in the light, in the beautiful light of God! Walk in the light, in the

light!.......................... Walk........................ in the
beau-ti-ful light of God! Walk in the light in the

light!..................... Walk in the beau-ti-ful light of God.
beau-ti-ful light of God!

FLOATING IN ON THE TIDE OF TIME.

Rev. Johnson Oatman, Jr.   Adam Geibel.

1. Wea - ry with toil - ing and worn out with care, Soon I shall
2. Un - der the ban - ner of Je - sus I've fought, With Him the
3. Out on the mountain of sin once was I, No hope of
4. Work - ing for Je - sus I've stood for the right, Fear - ing no

en - ter those por - tals so fair; Long years I've strug - gled and
lost sheep of Is - rael I've sought, Shout - ed His prais - es a -
heav - en, and fear - ing to die; But Je - sus called me, and
dan - ger where thick was the fight; Life's gold - en noon - tide I've

fought a - gainst sin, Now I have noth - ing to do but float in.
bove bat - tle's din, Now I have noth - ing to do but float in.
par - doned all sin, Now I have noth - ing to do but float in.
giv - en to Him, Now I have noth - ing to do but float in-

Chorus.

Float - ing in— right in— on the tide of time, Float - ing

in— right in—where the bright stars shine, Floating in— right in— on the

waves so cold, Float-ing in— right in— to the streets of gold.

TURN TO THE LORD.

JOSEPH HART.

ANON.
FINE.

1. { Come, ye sin-ners, poor and need-y, Weak and wounded, sick and sore;
   { Je-sus read-y stands to save you, Full of pit-y, love, and pow'r.
D.C.—Glo-ry, hon-or, and sal-va-tion, Christ, the Lord, has come to reign.

CHORUS.

D.C.

Turn to the Lord and seek sal-va-tion, Sound the praise of His dear name;

2. Now, ye needy, come and welcome,
   God's free bounty glorify;
   True belief and true repentance,
   Every grace that brings you nigh.

3. Let not conscience make you linger,
   Nor of fitness fondly dream;

All the fitness He requireth,
Is to feel your need of Him.

4. Come, ye weary, heavy-laden,
   Bruised and mangled by the fall,
   If you tarry till you're better,
   You will never come at all.

144 ON TO VICTORY.

E. A. H.

Rev. Elisha A. Hoffman.

1. Christian, gird the arm-or on, There's a vic-t'ry to be won
2. Let his ban-ner be unfurled Till it waves o'er all the world,
3. When the bat-tle shall be done, And the vic-to-ry be won,
4. That will be an hour of joy, Praise shall then our tongues employ,

For the Lord, for the Lord; Take the helmet, sword and shield,
Sea to sea, shore to shore; Till the na-tions all shall own
Con-flict past, con-flict past; In the new Je-ru-sa-lem
More and more, more and more; We shall stand before the King,

Forth un-to the bat-tle-field At his word, at his word.
He is King, and he a-lone, Ev-er-more, ev-er-more.
We shall wear a di-a-dem At the last, at the last.
And the song of triumph sing Ev-er-more, ev-er-more.

CHORUS.

On we'll march....... to vic-to-ry, Je-sus will our leader
On we'll march....... to vic-to-ry, To a fi-nal and a
On we'll march to vic-to-ry,

1
be, Je-sus will our lead-er be; :‖ glorious vic-to-ry.
2

RICH IN BLESSING.

JAS. ALLEN.
Fervently.

GEO. C. HUGG.

1. Sweet the moments, rich in blessing, Which be-fore the cross I spend;
2. Tru - ly bless - ed is this sta-tion, Low be-fore His cross to lie,
3. Here it is I find my heaven, While up - on the Lamb I gaze;
4. Love and grief my heart di-vid-ing, With my tears His feet I bathe;

Life and health, and peace possesing, From the sin-ner's dy - ing Friend.
While I see di-vine compassion, Beam-ing from His lov-ing eye.
Love I much, I've much forgiven; I'm a mir - a - cle of grace.
Con-stant still in faith a - bid-ing, Life de - riv - ing from His death.

CHORUS.

Rich in blessing! rich in blessing! Moments at the cross I spend;

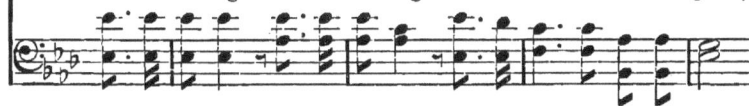

Tru - ly bless-ed is this sta-tion, Low be-fore the cross to bend.

LIFE'S PILGRIMAGE.

(Responsive Duet.)

BIRDIE BELL.   J. HOWARD ENTWISLE.

1ST VOICE.

1. "Pilgrim, trav - el-stain'd and wea - ry, Pressing on   with way-worn
2. "Pilgrim, art   thou sad - ly weeping? Dim with watch - ing   are thine
3. "Courage, pil - grim, o'er thee bending, Bands of an - gels watch in

feet,   Is the jour - ney long and dreary? Do the temp - ests round thee beat?"
eyes? Anxious vig - il art thou keeping, Looking for   the glad sun-rise?"
love; From the temp-ter's wile's de-fending, Onward press and look a - bove!"

2ND VOICE.

"Ah, my friend,   why should I sor - row? End-less joy   a - waits my
"Friend, I some - times catch a glim - mer, Of the Cit - y's jas - per
"Friend, no e - vil am I fear - ing, Je-sus guides me all the

soul, On some dis - tant, glad - some mor - row, I shall
wall, And that ra - diant, pear - ly shim - mer, Well re -
way, Yes, my feet are dai - ly near - ing, That fair

Rit. ad lib.......................................

reach the bless - ed Goal. On some dis - tant, glad-some
pays my soul for all. And that ra - diant, pear - ly
Land of change-less day! Yes, my feet are dail - ly

mor - row, I shall reach the bless - ed goal."
shim - mer, Well re - pays my soul for all."
near - ing, That fair Land of change-less day!"

ARE YOU WASHED IN THE BLOOD?

E. A. H.

Rev. Elisha A. Hoffman.

1. Have you been to Je-sus for the cleansing pow'r? Are you
2. Are you walk-ing dai-ly by the Saviour's side? Are you
3. When the Bridegroom com-eth, will your robes be white, Pure and
4. Lay a-side the garments that are stained with sin, And be

washed in the blood of the Lamb? Are you ful-ly trusting in his
washed in the blood of the Lamb? Do you rest each moment in the
white in the blood of the Lamb? Will your soul be read-y for the
washed in the blood of the Lamb; There's a fountain flowing for the

CHORUS.

grace this hour? Are you washed in the blood of the Lamb?
cru-ci-fied? Are you washed in the blood of the Lamb?
mansions bright, And be washed in the blood of the Lamb?
soul un-clean, O be washed in the blood of the Lamb.

Are you

washed in the blood, In the soul-cleansing blood of the Lamb? Are your
Are you washed in the blood, of the Lamb?

garments spotless? Are they white as snow? Are you washed in the blood of the Lamb?

YE DOORS LIFT UP YOUR PORTALS.

Rev. Johnson Oatman, Jr.　　　　　　　　　　　　W. F. Fowler.

With animation.

1. Ye doors lift up your por - tals, Lift up your heads, ye gates, While angels tell to mor-tals What joy for them a-waits. They tell them of a stran-ger Who just from glo-ry came; "He lies in yonder man-ger, And Je-sus is his name." Al - le - lu - ia, al-le-lu - ia, Praise the Lord!

2. Then o - ver plain and field - wide Appeared a star so bright That ev'-ry vale and hill-side Were flooded with its light; While sweeter than the ring-ing Of chimes of sil-ver bells The notes of an-gels, sing-ing, O'er all the woodland swells. Al - le - lu - ia, al-le-lu - ia, Praise the Lord!

3. Roll on the wondrous sto - ry A-bout the Saviour's birth, For when he came from glo - ry The heavens kissed the earth. Once more we find the Gar-den Of E- den there restored, For Christ brought peace and par-don And fav - or with the Lord. Al - le - lu - ia, al-le-lu - ia, Praise the Lord!

GALILEE.

ROBERT MORRIS, LL. D.

GEO. C. HUGG.

Slow and feelingly.

1. Each coo-ing dove............... and sigh-ing bough,...............
2. Each flowr'-y glen............... and mos-sy dell, ...
3. And when I read............... the thrill-ing love,...............

Each coo-ing dove -
Each flowr'y glen
And when I read

and sigh-ing bough,
and mos-sy dell,
the thrill-ing love,

That makes the eve................... so blest to me,...............
Where hap-py birds................... in song a-gree, ...
Of Him who walked................... up-on the sea,...............

That makes the eve
Where hap-py birds
Of Him who walked

so blest to me,
in song a-gree,
up-on the sea,

Has some-thing far................... di-vin-er now,...............
Thro' sun-ny morn .... the prais-es tell,...............
I long, O, how................... I long once more,......... ....

Has something far
Thro' sun-ny morn
I long, O, how

di-vin-er now,
the prais-es tell,
I long once more,

It bears me back................... to Gal-i-lee,...............
Of sights, and sounds................. in Gal-i-lee,...............
To fol-low Him................... in Gal-i-lee,...............

It bears me back
Of sights, and sounds
To fol-low Him

to Gal-i-lee,
in Gal-i-lee,
in Gal-i-lee,

REFRAIN.

O Gal - i - lee,.................... sweet Gal - i - lee,....................
O Gal - i - lee, sweet Gal - i - lee,

Where Je - sus loved.................. so much to be,.....................
Where Je - sus loved so much to be,

O Gal - i - lee,.................... sweet Gal - i - lee,....................
O Gal - i - lee, sweet Gal - i - lee,

rall.

Come sing thy song..................... a - gain to me....................
Come sing thy song a - gain to me.

I EXPECT TO GET TO HEAVEN BY THE SAME OLD WAY.

Rev. Johnson Oatman, Jr.

Geo. C. Hugg.

1. The way our fa-ther's trav-eled is good e-nough for me,
2. The world may sneer and tell me I'll nev-er reach the goal,
3. When bowers of sin en-tice me to rest my wea-ry feet,
4. Mill-ions are now in glo-ry, in shin-ing white ar-rayed,

They fol-lowed in the foot-steps that led from Cal-va-ry,
That good works are suf-fi-cient to save a hu-man soul,
I find in Christ my Sav-iour, a safe, a sure re-treat,
Who trav-eled this same path-way, and oft-en were dis-mayed,

It led them up to glo-ry, that land of end-less day,
But while the world is talk-ing, I still will watch and pray,
He tells me to press on-ward, and not look back, nor stay,
But hap-py now in glo-ry they sing both night and day,

I ex-pect to get to heav-en by the same old way.
I ex-pect to get to heav-en by the same old way.
I ex-pect to get to heav-en by the same old way.
I ex-pect to get to heav-en by the same old way.

I EXPECT TO GET TO HEAVEN, etc. Concluded.

CHORUS.

O this bless-ed old way, it is good e-nough for me,

Ritard.

It is good e-nough for me, it is good e-nough for me;

a tempo.

My Sav-iour goes be-fore me, I fol-low Him each day,

I ex-pect to get to heav-en by the same old way.

PRAISE YE THE LORD.

E. E. HEWITT.   FLORENCE W. WILLIAMS.

1. Praise ye, the Lord, an - gels of light! Sing, shin - ing host, from the
2. Praise ye the Lord, sweet, blushing flow'rs, While happy songs ring from
3. Praise ye the Lord, child-ren of men! Come, with re - joic - ing, re -

blest heav'n - ly height; Praise ye the Lord, sun, moon, and star,
green wood-land bow'rs; Praise ye the Lord, fair sum-mer glow,
ech - o the strain; Praise ye the Lord, let songs of love

Show forth His praise, near and far, Praise ye the Lord,
Praise Him, ye soft fall - ing snow! Praise ye the Lord,
Blend with the voic - es a - bove, Praise ye the Lord,

bright, jewelled sky, Hon - or and glo - ry to Thee, O Most High!
moun - tains and hills, Grand roll-ing bil - lows, and mur-mur - ing rills.
sing, Zi - on, sing, Trust Him for - ev - er, our Sav-iour and King.

CHORUS.

O praise the Lord,.................. ye sons of light !..................
O praise the Lord, ye sons of light !

Praise Him a - bove,..................... in glo - ry bright ;...............
Praise Him a-bove, in glo - ry bright ;

Praise Him be - low,................... ho - san - nas bring,................
Praise Him be-low, ho-san - nas bring,

Ex - alt and mag - ni - fy our bless - ed King.................
our bless-ed King.

ETERNITY'S SHORE.

To Rev. H. D. Lowing.

Adam Geibel.   Adam Geibel.

SOLO AND QUARTETTE.

1. There's a mansion just o - ver the riv - er, Which my Sav-iour's preparing for
2. In that mansion just o - ver the riv - er, Where the saints of all a - ges re -
3. When the jour-ney of life is com-ple - ted, When its toil and its warfare is

me;.......... And I know I shall rest there for - ev - er, When I've
- pose;......... There the Lamb is resplend-ent for - ev - er, For the
done;......... When the light of its day is re-cede-ing, And I

cross'd o'er the dark, nar-row sea;.......... And I know I shall meet ma-ny
light of His pur - i - ty glows;........ O I'm longing, and watching, and
bask in its last set-ting sun;.......... Then dear Je - sus, I pray Thee pre -

lov'd ones,   Who have cross'd the dark wa- ters be - fore;   And the
wait -'ing,   And my heart yearns to go, more and more;   Ah! what
- pare me,   That to man-sions of bliss I may soar;   And to

Sav-iour I'll see in His glo - ry,   When I land on E - ter - ni - ty's shore.
joy and what rap-ture will greet me,   When I land on E - ter - ni - ty's shore.
Thee will I give all the glo - ry,   When I land on E - ter - ni - ty's shore.

REFRAIN.
mf   *cres.*

When I land on E - ter - ni - ty's shore, When I land on E - ter - ni - ty's shore;

f   *dim.*   *rit.*   *p*

Yes, the Saviour I'll see in His glo - ry, When I land on e - ter - ni - ty's shore.

HEAR US WHILE WE PRAY.

Rev. Johnson Oatman, Jr.

Geo. C. Hugg.

1. Sav - iour we come to Thee this hour, Need - ing Thy grace,
2. Sav - iour speak peace to ev - 'ry heart, Calm ev - 'ry breast
3. Sav - iour be Thou our friend and guide, Cast out all sin,
4. Sav - iour reach out to us Thy hand, With - out Thy help

need - ing Thy pow'r; Close by Thee we would ev - er stay,
be - fore we part; Turn all our dark - ness in - to day,
cast out all pride; Teach us Thy man - dates to o - bey,
we can - not stand; Lead us to realms of end - less day,

CHORUS.

O Sav - iour hear us while we pray.
O Sav - iour hear us while we pray.
O Sav - iour hear us while we pray.
O Sav - iour hear us while we pray.

O Sav - iour hear us while we

pray, Draw near, and turn us not a - way; Poor, need - y,
while we pray, not a - way;

weak, we come to Thee to-day, O Sav - iour hear us while we pray.

JESUS, I MY CROSS HAVE TAKEN.

Henry Francis Lyte.

1. Je - sus, I my cross have tak - en, All to leave and fol - low Thee;
2. Let the world de - spise and leave me; They have left my Sav - iour too;
3. Haste thee on from grace to glo - ry, Armed by faith and winged by pray'r;

Des - ti - tute, de - spised, for - sak - en, Thou from hence my all shalt be;
Human hearts and looks deceive me; Thou art not, like men, un - true;
Heav'n's e - ter - nal day's be - fore thee, God's own hand shall guide thee there;

Per - ish ev - 'ry fond am - bi - tion, All I've sought and hoped and known,
And while thou shalt smile up - on me, God of wis - dom, love and might,
Soon shall close thine earthly mis - sion, Soon shall pass thy pil - grim days;

Yet how rich is my con - di - tion! God and heav'n are still my own.
Foes may hate, and friends may shun me, Show Thy face and all is bright.
Hope shall change to glad fru - i - tion, Faith to sight, and pray'r to praise.

160 THE WRITING ON THE WALL.

REV. JOHNSON OATMAN, JR.   ADAM GEIBEL.

1. Once king Bel-chaz-zar gave a feast, To no-bles great and grand,
2. Fresh cour-age take, God is your friend, Tho' en - e-mies may shout,
3. Who would be tru - ly great and grand, To sin can-not af - ford,

From North to South, from West to East, They came from all the land;
He will go with you to the end, Your foes will put to rout;
For they a-lone se-cure-ly stand, Who trust in God the Lord;

God's ho - ly ves - sels were brought in, A shout went up from all,
Tho' wick - ed men may flour - ish here, Like Bay trees green and tall,
Be sure to stand up for the right, The wrong will sure - ly fall,

But there appeared, to check this sin, The Writ - ing on the Wall.
What tells us they will dis - ap-pear? The Writ - ing on the Wall.
For see, in let - ters clear as light, The Writ - ing on the Wall.

CHORUS.

The Church of God shall ev - er stand, Her en - e-mies shall fall;

THE WRITING ON THE WALL. Concluded. 161

For God has put with His own hand, The Writing on the Wall.

REJOICE AND BE GLAD.

H. BONAR.   J. J. HUSBAND.

1. Re-joice and be glad: the Re-deem-er has come; Go look on His
2. Re-joice and be glad: for the blood has been shed; Re-demption is
3. Re-joice and be glad: for the Lamb that was slain, O'er death is tri-
4. Re-joice and be glad: for our King is on high; He pleadeth for
5. Re-joice and be glad: for He com-eth a-gain, He com-eth in

REFRAIN.

cra-dle, His cross, and His tomb.
finished, the price has been paid.
umphant, and liv-eth a-gain. } Sound His praises, tell the sto-ry, Of
us on His throne in the sky.
glo-ry, the Lamb that was slain.

Him who was slain; Sound His praises, tell with gladness, He liv-eth a-gain.

For last verse.—He com-eth a-gain.

THERE'S A MANSION OVER YONDER.

IDA L. REED.   ADAM GEIBEL.

SOLO OR QUARTETTE.

1. There's a man-sion o - ver yon-der, Long a - go pre-pared for me,
2. There no trou-bled wea - ry warrings, Shall my heart with sor - row fill,

Read - y wait-ing for my com-ing, By the shin - ing crys-tal sea;
Earth-ly griefs are past for - ev - er, Ev - 'ry pain and ev - 'ry ill;

Earth - ly homes too soon will crumble, Here I wan - der to and fro,
There's a man - sion, o - ver yon-der, Home of sweet e - ter - nal rest,

But this stand-eth sure for - ev - er, I its end-less peace shall know.
. Read - y wait-ing for my com-ing, In the Cit - y of the blest.

THERE'S A MANSION OVER YONDER. Concluded.

CHORUS.

There's a man-sion for me wait-ing. O - ver yon - der on the shore,

By my Father's hands twas builded, It is mine for - ev - er more.

LABAN.

HEATH.

LOWELL MASON.

1. My soul, be on thy guard, Ten thous-and foes a - rise;
2. Oh, watch, and fight and pray, The bat - tle ne'er give o'er;
3. Ne'er think the vic - t'ry won, Nor lay thine arm - or down;
4. Fight on, my soul, till death Shall bring thee to thy God;

The hosts of sin are press-ing hard To draw thee from the skies.
Re - new it bold-ly ev - 'ry day, And help di - vine im - plore.
Thy arduous work will not be done Till thou ob - tain the crown.
He'll take thee, at thy part-ing breath Up to His blest a - bode.

BEAUTIFUL LAND WITH JASPER WALLS.

Rev. Johnson Oatman, Jr.   Geo. C. Hugg.

Slow, and expressive.

1. There's a   beau - ti - ful land that a - waits the just, When these
2. There the an - gel's are twang - ing their harps of gold, Sing - ing
3. There the ran - somed are sing - ing re - demp - tion's song, And the
4. To that beau - ti - ful land   I will some - time go, Where love,

bod - ies of clay have re - turned to dust, Don't you see o'er the riv - er those
o - ver the sto - ry that ne'er grows old, They are rais - ing glad shouts while the
cho - rus is ring - ing both loud and strong, Of the blood that for - ev - er from
joy, and sweet peace will eternally flow, With my Je - sus I'll dwell where no

state - ly   halls? In that beau - ti - ful land with the Jas - per walls.
har - mo - ny falls, In that beau - ti - ful land with the Jas - per walls.
Cal - va - ry calls, To that beau - ti - ful land with the Jas - per walls.
e - vil be - falls, In that beau - ti - ful land with the Jas - per walls.

CHORUS.

O that beau - ti - ful land, that beau - ti - ful land, I've a home o - ver

BEAUTIFUL LAND, etc. Concluded.

165

there at the Lord's right-hand; I've a man - sion se - cure when this

poor tent falls, In that beau-ti-ful land of the Jas-per walls.

WHEN THE POWER CAME DOWN.

JAMES STOCKTON. GEO. C. HUGG.

1. Once the Dis-ci-ples wait-ed, Once the Dis-ci-ples wait-ed;
2. Then Pe-ter preach'd a ser-mon, Then Pe-ter preach'd a ser-mon;
3. Once my poor heart was hea-vy, Once my poor heart was heav-vy;
4. We had a great re-vi-val, We had a great re-vi-val;
5. It made old Sa-tan trem-ble, It made old Sa-tan trem-ble;
6. I left the world be-hind me, I left the world be-hind me;

D. C.—Like wind with rush-ing might-y, Came down the Ho-ly Spir-it;

D.C. FINE.

'Twas in the up-per cham-ber, When the pow'r came down.
Three thou-sand were con-ver-ted, When the pow'r came down.
But Je-sus took my bur-den, When the pow'r came down.
And ma-ny were con-ver-ted, When the pow'r came down.
Be-cause his chain was bro-ken, When the pow'r came down.
I start-ed out for glo-ry, When the pow'r came down.

O there was great re-joic-ing, When the pow'r came down.

PRECIOUS LOVE OF JESUS.

Geo. C. Hugg.   Geo. C. Hugg.

1. The pre-cious love of Je - sus! It sav - eth e - ven me,
2. The pre-cious love of Je - sus! I'm hap - py all day long,
3. The pre-cious love of Je - sus! It fills my soul with joy;

It ran-somed me from fol - ly, And gave me lib - er - ty;
My soul is sweet-ly sing-ing, And Je - sus is my song;
It brings me peace and com - fort, And bliss with-out al - loy;

The pre - cious love of Je - sus! I'll sing the vic - to - ry,
The pre - cious love of Je - sus! 'Twill bear me safe - ly o'er,
The pre - cious love of Je - sus! I prize it more and more,

O glo - ry, hal - le - lu - jah! From sin I am set free.
A - cross the chill - ing riv - er, To Ca - naan's peaceful shore.
It cheers me on my jour - ney, To - ward the shin - ing shore.

CHORUS.

O the pre-cious love of Je-sus, It sav-eth e-ven

me, Sav-eth e-ven me, Sav-eth e-ven me,

Oh, the pre-cious love of Je-sus! It sav-eth e-ven me,

Glo-ry, glo-ry, hal-le-lu-jah! It sav-eth e-ven me.

*Chorus arranged from a Spiritual.

LAND BEYOND THE JORDAN.

ISAAC WATTS.   W. A. OGDEN.

1. There is a land of pure de - light, Where
2. Sweet fields be - yond the swell - ing flood, Stand
3. Oh, could we make our doubts re - move, Those

saints im - mor - tal reign; In - fi - nite day ex -
dress'd in liv - ing green! So to the Jews old
gloom - y doubts that rise, And see the Ca - naan

cludes the night, And pleas - ures ban - ish pain. There
Ca - naan stood, While Jor - dan rolled be - tween. But
that we love, With un - be - cloud - ed eyes. Could

ev - er - last - ing spring a - bides, And nev - er withering flow'rs;
timorous mor - tals start and shrink, To cross this nar - row sea,
we but climb where Mo - ses stood, And view the landscape o'er,

Death,like a nar-row sea di-vides, This heav'nly land from ours.
And lin-ger, shivering, on the brink,And fear to launch a-way.
Not Jor-dan's stream,nor death's cold flood, Should fright us from the shore.

CHORUS.

Land so bright and ver - nal, Land of spring e - ter - nal;

We long to gain Thy gold - en shore, Where lov'd ones meet to

part no more: Land of spring e - ter - nal.

WHEN WE ALL SHALL GATHER HOME.

IDA L. REED.   GEO. C. HUGG.

Fervently, not too fast.

1. When we all shall gath - er home, What re - joic - ing there will be;
2. When we all shall gath - er home, Friend meet friend beyond the tide;
3. When we all shall gath - er home, To that hap - py realm a - bove;

On that sun - ny gold - en shore, There be - side the crys - tal sea.
Oh what glad-ness will be mine, O - ver on the far - ther side.
What re - joic - ing there will be, Crown'd with sweet e - ter - nal love.

CHORUS.

When we all shall gath - er home, To that land of peace and rest,

What re-joic-ing there will be, 'Mid the mansions of the blest, Gath-er home,...... gath-er home,...... Gath-er home to die no more; Gath-er

Gather home, gather home, die no more,

Rit...

home,...... gath-er home,...... On that sun-ny gold-en shore.

Gather home, gather home,

REPENTANCE.

ROB'T FINCH.

1. Lord, I ap-proach the mer - cy - seat, Where Thou dost answer pray'r;
2. Thy prom-ise is my on - ly plea, With this I ven - ture nigh;
3. Bow'd down beneath a load of sin, By Sa - tan sore - ly press'd;
4. Be Thou my shield and hid - ing-place, That, shelter'd near Thy side;
5. O, wondrous love!—to bleed and die, To bear the cross and shame,

There humbly fall be - fore Thy feet,—For none can per - ish there.
Thou call-est bur-den'd souls to Thee, And such, O Lord, am I.
By wars with-out, and fears with-in, I come to Thee for rest.
I may re-joice in Je - sus' grace, In Je - sus cru - ci - fied.
That guil - ty sin - ners, such as I, Might plead Thy gracious Name.

THE KING'S PALACE.

BIRDIE BELL.   J. HOWARD ENTWISLE.

SOLO AND QUARTETTE.

1. O beau-ti-ful pal-ace up yon-der! We dream of thy glo-ries un-
2. O won-der-ful pal-ace up yon-der! Thy gate-ways of shimmering
3. O safe-sheltered pal-ace up yon-der! Tempta-tions may vex nev-er-

told,   We long for a glimpse of thy splen-dor, Thy rich-es of
light,   Thro' which pass the host of the ran-somed, Ar-rayed in pure
more,   Earth's sor-row-ful tri-als all o-ver, Sin nev-er can

jas-per and   gold;   To gaze thro' the heaven-ly por-tal, Where
garments of   white;   From earth's farthest borders they gath-er, Be-
pass thro' thy door;   The re-fuge of peace, strong, e-ter-nal, The

dwell - eth our Sav - iour and King,......... And list to the
- fore the great throne of the King,......... And join in a
pal - ace of Je - sus our King,......... May all of us

glo - ri - ous an - them, Which ju - bi-lant chor - is - ters sing.........
mar - vel - ous cho - rus, A song which no mor-tal can sing.........
en - ter thy por - tal, And heav-en's own mel - o-dies sing.........

CHORUS.

No mor-tal can gaze on thy splendor, O pal-ace of Je-sus our king,......

of Jesus our king,

No sing- er of earth can a - wak - en, The song which thy choristers sing.

CHEERING LIGHT.

Arranged.

Geo. C. Hugg.

1. There are bright shin - ing lights in the ha - ven,
2. There are lights by the shore as we jour - ney,
3. Oh, they tell of a hope that will cheer us,

Where my ves - sel 'mid per - ils I steer;
As we float down the riv - er of time;
In the 'midst of our sor - rows and cares;

And they gleam e - ven bright - er and bright - er
All the days of our pil - grim - age bright - en
When the lamp of our ves - sel burns dim - ly,

As that glo - ri - ous Cit - y I near.
With a ra - di - ance tru - ly sub - lime.
And we watch for the glim - mer of theirs.

CHORUS.

Light! Light! Light! Cheer-ing light from Fair Zi - on I see;

While my soul sings with rap - ture, Ho - san - na!

Ho - san - na! Lov - ing voi - ces are call - ing to me;

Hear them, sing - ing, On the strand by the bright Jas - per sea!

WONDERFUL BIBLE.

E. E. HEWITT.   ADAM GEIBEL.

1. Won - der - ful Bi - ble, Book of all a - ges, Gift of our
2. Won - der - ful Bi - ble, beau - ti - ful sto - ry, Sto - ry of
3. Won - der - ful Bi - ble! none ev - er per - ish Heed - ing its
4. Won - der - ful Bi - ble, bless - ed pos-sess - ion, Let us up -

Fath - er, sent from a - bove, Life ev - er - last - ing beams from its
Je - sus, Sav-iour of men; Dy - ing for sin - ners, plead-ing in
coun - sels, led by its light; Ev -'ry sweet prom-ise, O let us
- hold it, home and a - broad; Ser-vants of Je - sus, this be our

pag - es, Peace be - yond meas - ure, mer - cy and love.
glo - ry, Hear it with glad - ness, tell it a - gain.
cher - ish, Till Heav-en's morn - ing end earth - ly night.
mis - sion, Send to the need - y, ti - dings from God.

CHORUS.

Won - der - ful Bi - ble, Book of sal - va - tion, Tell - ing of mer - cy, breathing of love; Won-der-ful Bi - ble, God's re - vel -

- a - tion, Show-ing His chil - dren, man-sions a - bove.

JESUS, SAVIOUR, PILOT ME.

REV. EDWARD HOPPER, D. D.   J. E. GOULD.

1. Je - sus, Sav - iour, pi - lot me, O - ver Life's tempestuous sea,
2. As a moth - er stills her child, Thou canst hush the o - cean wild;
3. When at last I near the shore, And the fear - ful breakers roar

Un-known waves around me roll, Hid - ing rock and treach'rous shoal,
Boist'rious waves o - bey Thy will, When Thou say - est "peace be still;"
'Twixt me and my peaceful rest, Then while lean - ing on Thy breast,

Chart and com - pass come from Thee, Je - sus, Sav - iour, pi - lot me.
Wond'rous sov' - reign of the sea, Je - sus, Sav - iour, pi - lot me.
May I hear Thee say to me, "Fear not, I will pi - lot thee."

WHAT IS THAT TO THEE.

JOHN 21: 22.

REV. JOHNSON OATMAN, JR.   GEO. C. HUGG.

Not too fast.

1. Pe - ter asked the Sav-iour, "What shall this man do?" Standing on the
2. Je - sus left a mes-sage to tell ev-'ry one, E - ven those who
3. Nev - er wait for oth - ers when there's work for you, Lis - ten to the
4. Nic - o - de - mus heard, "Ye must be born a - gain," But he answered
5. You must work for Je - sus, you must watch and pray, Hear His man-date,

shore of Gal - i - lee,   "I   have got   to suf - fer, will John
live be-yond the sea,   Do   not stop   to ques - tion if   this
voice from Gal - i - lee,   Do   not ask   like Pe - ter "What shall
"How can these things be?"   Nev - er ques - tion like him, "how?" or
"Rise and fol - low me,"   Do   not stop   and ques - tion, when He

Slow...................

suf - fer too?"   But   He   an-swered, "What   is   that   to thee."
should be done, Hear the   an - swer, "What   is   that   to thee."
this man do,"   Hear the   an - swer, "What   is   that   to thee."
"Why?" or "When?" Hear the   an - swer, "What   is   that   to thee."
speaks o - bey,   For He   an - swers, "What   is   that   to thee."

CHORUS.

What is that to thee, O what is that to thee, There is work that

WHAT IS THAT TO THEE. Concluded.

none can do but thee; Nev - er stop to ask what oth - er's

Slow

work shall be, Hear the an - swer, "What is that to thee."

JUST AS I AM.

CHARLOTTE ELLIOTT.   WM. B. BRADBURY.

1. Just as I am, with-out one plea, But that Thy blood was shed for me,
2. Just as I am, and wait-ing not To rid my soul of one dark blot,
3. Just as I am, tho' toss'd a-bout With many a conflict, many a doubt,
4. Just as I am—poor, wretched, blind, Sight, rich-es, heal-ing of the mind,
5. Just as I am—Thou wilt re-ceive, Wilt welcome, pardon, cleanse, relieve;
6. Just as I am—Thy love unknown Hath bro-ken ev-'ry bar-rier down;

And that Thou bidd'st me come to Thee, O Lamb of God, I come! I come!
To Thee whose blood can cleanse each spot, O Lamb of God, I come! I come!
Fightings within, and fears without, O Lamb of God, I come! I come!
Yea, all I need, in Thee to find, O Lamb of God, I come! I come!
Be - cause Thy promise I be-lieve, O Lamb of God, I come! I come!
Now, to be Thine, yea, Thine alone, O Lamb of God, I come! I come!

KATE CAMERON. LABAN SOLOMON.

SOLO. 1st. VOICE.

1. Trav'ler, with - er art thou go - ing, Heedless of the clouds that form?
2. Trav'ler, art thou here a stranger, Not to fear the tempest's pow'r?
3. Trav'ler, now a moment lin-ger, Soon the dark - ness will be o'er;
4. Trav'ler, yon - der nar-row por-tal O-pens to re-ceive thy form;

ACCOMP. mp

2nd VOICE.

Naught to me the wind's rough blowing, Mine's a land without a storm;
I have not a tho't of dan - ger, Tho' the sky more darkly lower,
No! I see a beck'ning fin - ger, Guid-ing to a far-off shore;
Yes! and I shall be im-mor - tal In that land without a storm;

rall. e cres.

And I'm go - ing, yes, I'm go - ing, To that land that has no storm;
For I'm go - ing, yes, I'm go - ing, To that land that has no storm;
And I'm go - ing, yes, I'm go - ing, To that land that has no storm;
And I'm go - ing, yes, I'm go - ing, To that land that has no storm;

f rall. e cres.

tempo. p

I am go - ing, yes, I'm go - ing, To that land that has no storm.
. For I'm go - ing, yes, I'm go - ing, To that land that has no storm.
I am go - ing, yes, I'm go - ing, To that land that has no storm.
I am go - ing, yes, I'm go - ing, To that land that has no storm.

tempo. p

CHORUS.

We are go - ing, yes, we're go - ing, Soon the glo - rious day will dawn ;

We are go - ing, yes, we're go - ing To the land without a storm.

OLD HUNDRED. L. M.

G. FRANC.

1. Be-fore Je - ho-vah's aw - ful throne, Ye na-tions, bow with sa-cred joy;

Know that the Lord is God a - lone; He can cre - ate, and He de - stroy.

IT IS WONDERFUL.

REV. H. J. ZELLEY.   GEO. C. HUGG.

1. The bless-ed Son of God loves di - vine-ly,   He gave His life my soul
2. The bless-ed Son of God sweetly saves me,   His precious blood can cleanse
3. The bless-ed Son of God safe-ly keeps me,   He guards my soul from sin

to re - deem; Up-on His gen - tle breast now re - clin-ing,   I'm
from all sin; His "New Name" on my heart He is writ-ing,   His
ev - 'ry day; The eye that watch-es me nev - er slumbers,   He

bask-ing in the love-light su-preme; His love is tend-'rer far, than a
Ho - ly Spir-it now dwells within; He gives me need -ed grace ev - 'ry
ev - er guides my steps, lest I stray; And I, when He is near, rest se -

mother's,   I know He'll never leave me to stray; I'll share with Him great
moment,   He shows to me the way I should take, I feel His gen-tle
cure-ly,   No weap-on that is made can pre-vail, My heart is full of

joy as I tread the upward path, For I always feel Him near when I pray.
hand as I'm walking by His side, And I know He'll never leave, nor forsake.
joy and I serve Him without fear, For I know His wondrous love cannot fail.

CHORUS.

O   it   is   won - der - ful,   O   it   is   won - der - ful,
O yes it   is   O yes it   is

Rallentando...............................

O   it is won-der-ful, How the bless-ed Je - sus loves me.
O yes it is

MAITLAND.

THOMAS SHEPHERD.   GEO. N. ALLEN.

1. Must Je - sus bear the cross a - lone, And all the world go free?
2. The   con - se - cra - ted cross I'll bear, Till death shall set me free?
3. Up - on the crys-tal pavement, down At Je - sus' pierced feet,
4. O   precious cross! O glorious crown! O res - ur - rec-tion day!

No, there's a cross for ev -'ry one, And there's a cross for me.
And then go home my crown to wear, For there's a crown for me.
With joy I'll cast my gold - en crown, And His dear name re - peat.
Ye   an- gels, from the stars come down, And bear my soul a - way.

O SINNER START FOR HOME.

REV. JOHNSON OATMAN, JR.   GEO. C. HUGG.

1. O there is great joy in heav-en when a sin-ner starts for home,
2. You have squandered time and money searching for the joys of earth,
3. But with-in your Father's dwelling there are joys that nev-er fade,
4. O come sin-ner, start for heav-en, do not wait an-oth-er day,

In the pres-ence of the an-gels we are told;
You have wand-ered far a-way in paths of sin;
There His ta-ble is spread dai-ly with the best;
For the au-gels wait to sound their ju-bi-lee;

For it makes the an-gels hap-py there to see him cease to roam,
But you've al-ways found a heart-ache, where you first ex-pec-ted mirth,
And while in the world you're starving, Lo! He longs to give you aid,
Your dear Fath-er waits and watch-es there, to meet you on the way,

And to view him start for shel-ter to God's fold.
You have nev-er found in this world peace with-in.
There He longs to fold you to His lov-ing breast.
Start for home, and help to swell their mel-o-dy.

CHORUS.

O sin - ner start for home, won't you start for home to - night? You have

wandered long a-bout this world so cold; The an-gels they are watching, O

what a bless-ed sight, They will shout to see you starting for the fold.

KING OF LOVE.

SIR H. W. BAKER.　　　　DR. J. B. DYKES.

1. The King of love my Shep-herd is, Whose goodness fail-eth nev - er;
2. Where streams of liv-ing wa - ter flow My ransom'd soul He lead-eth,
3. Per-verse and fool-ish, oft I stray'd, But yet in love He sought me,
4. In death's dark vale I fear no ill With Thee, dear Lord, be - side me,
5. And so, thro' all the length of days, Thy good-ness fail-eth nev - er;

I noth-ing lack if I am His, And He is mine for - ev - er.
And, where the ver-dant pas-tures grow, With food ce - les - tial feed-eth.
And on His shoul-der gent-ly laid, And home, re-joic - ing, brought me.
Thy rod and staff my com-fort still, Thy Cross be-fore to guide me.
Good Shepherd, may I sing Thy praise With - in Thy house for - ev - er.

"ALL'S WELL! ALL'S WELL!"

BIRDIE BELL.   J. HOWARD ENTWISLE.

SOLO. *With expression.*

1. No star shines o'er the rest - less seas, Yet on the ship doth
2. And so we sail up - on life's sea, Some-times the skies are
3. O heav'n-ly Pi - lot, be our guide, Up - on time's chang - ing

ride, We hear the moan - ing of the breeze, The
dark, No star the anx - ious eye can see, Waves
sea, When o'er the wa - ters smooth we glide, And

surg - ing of the tide; A sound breaks on the
toss our fra - gile bark; We shud - der at the
hearts are glad and free; Or when the skies grow

list - 'ning ear, The tink - ling of a bell, An
sad wind's sigh, It seems to sound our knell, But
dark a - bove, And high the bil - lows swell, Call

answ'ring voice our hearts doth cheer, It cries, "All's well! all's well."
O, we hear a bless - ed cry, The glad "All's well! all's well."
un - to us in tones of love, The sweet "All's well! all's well."

CHORUS. *Faster.*

rit................

f

All's well! all's well! A - bove the sound of wind and wave,
All's well, all's well,

m

p

We hear the cheer-y cry, "Be brave, O soul, all's well! all's well!
all's well!

JESUS OUR SAVIOUR.

REV. H. J. ZELLEY.   GEO. C. HUGG.

1. Je - sus, our Sav - iour, on er - rands of mer - cy, Went from the
2. Heal - ing the lep - ers who watch'd for His com - ing, In great com -
3. Tongues that were si - lent by His word were loosened, Limbs that were
4. Je - sus to - day is the same might - y Sav - iour, Con - quer - or

mount - ains to Gal - li - lee's wave; Ev - 'ry - where seek - ing the
pass - ion the mul - ti - tudes fed; Je - sus gave sight to the
use - less were made strong and well; Hearts stain'd with e - vil He
o - ver death, hell and the grave; Come to Him quick - ly and

poor and the need - y, Seek - ing to com - fort re - lieve and to save.
eyes that were blind - ed, Heal'd all the suffering and brought back the dead.
made pure and spot - less, Fill'd with thanksgiving His sto - ry to tell.
trust in Him ful - ly, Je - sus a - lone is the might - y to save.

CHORUS.

Won - der - ful Sav - iour, won - der - ful Sav - iour, Gen - tle and

ten - der and lov - ing and kind; All who re - ceive Him and ful - ly be-lieve Him, Par - don and cleansing and wis-dom may find.

MY JESUS, I LOVE THEE.

A. J. GORDON.

1. My Je - sus, I love Thee, I know Thou art mine; For Thee all the
2. I love Thee, be - cause Thou Hast first lov - ed me, And purchased my
3. I'll love Thee in life, I will love Thee in death, And praise Thee as
4. In man-sions of glo - ry And end - less de-light, I'll ev - er a -

fol - lies Of sin I re-sign; My gra-cious Re - deem - er, My
par - don On Cal - va-ry's tree; I love Thee for wear - ing The
long as Thou lend - est me breath; And say when the death - dew Lies
dore Thee In heav - en so bright; I'll sing with the glit - ter - ing

Sav - iour art Thou, If ev - er I loved Thee, My Je - sus, 'tis now.
thorns on Thy brow; If ev - er I loved Thee, My Je - sus, 'tis now.
cold on my brow, If ev - er I loved Thee, My Je - sus, 'tis now.
Crown on my brow, If ev - er I loved Thee, My Je - sus, 'tis now.

WHAT HAVE YOU DONE FOR JESUS?

REV. JOHNSON OATMAN, JR.   J. HOWARD ENTWISLE.

1. The ques-tion comes to you   to - day, What have you done for Je - sus?
2. With - in the har - vest fields of sin, What have you done for Je - sus?
3. There's work e - nough for all your days, What have you done for Je - sus?

If you are on the nar - row way, What have you done for   Je - sus?
Have you not one sheaf gathered in? What have you done for Je - sus?
While an - gel voic - es ring His praise, What have you done for Je - sus?

The Sav - iour has done much for you, He died to prove His friendship true,
While dy - ing men be - fore you stand, Can you not give a help - ing hand?
O do   not let this ques-tion go, Up - on it hangs your weal or woe,

Is there not something you can do? What have you done for   Je - sus?
Can you not point them to that land? What have you done for Je - sus?
The ques-tion is   not what you know, What have you done for   Je - sus?

WHAT HAVE YOU DONE, etc. Concluded.

CHORUS.

What have you done for Je - sus? What have you done for Je - sus?

There's work to do, there's work for you, What have you done for Je - sus?

BOYLSTON.

BENJ. BEDDOME.   LOWELL MASON.

1. Did Christ o'er sin - ners weep, And shall our cheeks be dry! Let
2. The Son of God in tears The wond'ring an - gels see; Be
3. He wept that we might weep—Each sin de-mands a tear; In

tears of pen - i - ten - tial grief Flow forth from ev - 'ry eye.
thou as - ton-ished, O my soul: He shed those tears for thee.
heav'n a - lone no sin is found, And there's no weep-ing there.

O GRANT ME ONE LOOK.

REV. JOHNSON OATMAN, JR.   J. HOWARD ENTWISLE.

Feelingly.

1. Dear Sav-iour, my soul is pant-ing for Thee, As hart for the
2. One look at Thy face would melt my poor heart, One look would be
3. O grant me dear Sav-iour one look at Thee, Then I shall be
4. O grant me dear Sav-iour one look at Thee, O let me look

clear wa-ter brook; I'm pant-ing, O Lord, Thy dear face to see,
all I could stand; One look at Thy wounds should cause tears to start,
spot-less with-in; For I shall be like Thee when thee I see,
to Thee and live; To see Thee, this earth a heaven would be,

CHORUS.

O grant me dear Sav-iour one look.
Like riv-ers that flow thro' the land.
Be sanc-ti-fied, free from all sin.
Just one look dear Sav-iour pray give.

O grant me one look dear

Sav-iour at Thee, One look at Thy hands and Thy feet; One look at Thy

O GRANT ME ONE LOOK. Concluded.

side that bled on the tree, One look at Thy dear face, so sweet.

ORTONVILLE. C. M.

P. DODDRIDGE.

DR. T. HASTINGS.

1. Je - sus, I love Thy charm-ing name, 'Tis mu - sic to mine
2. Yes, Thou art pre-cious to my soul, My trans-port and my
3. All that my ar-dent soul can wish In Thee doth rich - ly
4. Thy grace shall dwell up - on my heart, And shed its frag - rance

ear; Fain would I sound it out so loud, That
trust; Jew - els to Thee are gaud - y toys, And
meet; Nor to my eyes is light so dear, Nor
there; The no - blest balm of all its wounds, The

all the earth might hear, That all the earth might hear.
gold is sor - did dust, And gold is sor - did dust.
friend-ship half so sweet, Nor friend - ship half so sweet.
cor - dial of its care, The cor - dial of its care.

MY MOTHER'S HANDS.

MRS. M. E. W.   MRS. M. E. WILLSON.
Slow and with great expression.   Sister of the late P. P. BLISS. By per.

1. Oh, those beautiful, beautiful hands! Tho' they neither were white nor small,
2. Oh, those beautiful, beautiful hands! How they cared for my in-fant days!
3. Oh, those beautiful, beautiful hands! As they pressed my ach - ing brow;
4. Oh, those beautiful, beautiful hands! Thin and wrinkled with age they grew;
5. Oh, those beautiful, beautiful hands! I   stood by her cof-fin one day,
6. Oh, those beautiful, beautiful hands! I shall clasp them a-gain once more,

Yet my mother's hands were the fair - est, And love-li-est hands of all.
They guided my feet into pleasant paths, And smoothed all the rugged ways.
They cooled the fever and eased the pain, Me-thinks I can feel them now.
But still they toiled on for the child so dear, And her love seemed more tender and true.
And I kissed those hands so cold and white, As   qui- et and peaceful she lay.
As my feet touch the bank of the heav'nly land; We shall meet on that shining shore.

CHORUS.

My mother's dear hands, her beautiful hands, Which guided me safe o'er life's sands,

I   bless God's name for the mem'ry Of mother's own beau- ti - ful hands.

ACROSS THE BLUE.

Rev. Johnson Oatman, Jr.   Geo. C. Hugg.

1. Beyond the stars our loved ones wait, And watch for us   be- side the gate;
2. We long to join our loved ones there, And with them breathe on heaven's air
3. When we shall reach the streets of gold, We will our Saviour's face be- hold;
4. Then let us work and do our best, Soon God will take us home to rest;
5. Till then my soul   be still and wait, Soon thou wilt pass the pear- ly gate;

They wait for me, they watch for you, In that fair land   a- cross the blue.
The song that is   for - ev - er new, In glo - ry land, a- cross the blue.
We'll kiss the hand that led us thro' To mansions fair   a- cross the blue.
For if   he finds us tried and true, We'll live with him a- cross the blue.
Then what a meet- ing will en- sue With those we love a- cross the blue.

CHORUS.

A- cross the blue, a - cross the blue, From Pisgah's height be- hold the view;

Friends wait for me and watch for you, In sin- less land, a- cross the blue.

At a memorial service, held at Chester Heights Camp Meeting, Aug. 2, 1897, a great wave of religious enthusiasm passed over the audience when Rev. C. M. Boswell said, concerning Rev. Wm. Swindells, D. D., "He is away from us to-day, but he is just across the blue awaiting the time for us to come and greet him there. Let us send him word that we will be sure to come."

GOOD-BYE.

(PARTING HYMN.)

REV. JOHNSON OATMAN, JR.　　　　　　　　　　GEO. C. HUGG.

1. These scenes, so bright, now take their flight As birds in summer seem to fly;

2. As oft we meet, and dear ones greet, Heart speaks to heart and eye to eye;

3. Sometime we'll meet, sometime we'll greet Each other in that land on high;

A- gain we stand with parting hand, Good-bye, good-bye, good - bye.

Time speeds a- way, and soon we say, Good-bye, good-bye, good - bye.

There we will stay, and nev - er say, Good-bye, good-bye, good - bye.

CHORUS.

Good-bye, good-bye, we breathe a sigh, We say farewell with tear-dimmed eye;

God bless you all, God keep you all, Good-bye, good-bye, good - bye.

I'M GOING HOME AT LAST.

Rev. Johnson Oatman, Jr.

Adam Geibel.

1. When I see life's gold-en sun-set lighting up the ros-y West,
2. Tho' the road at times was wea-ry, o-ver which my feet have trod,
3. When I pass down thro' the val-ley and the shad-ow of the dead,

When the shadows backward o'er my way are cast; I shall look up-on that
Tho' thro' man-y trib-u-la-tions I have passed; Yet I soon will reach my
To my blessed Saviour's hand I will hold fast; He has promised to go

moment as the one supreme-ly blest, I'm go-ing home at last.
mansion in the cit-y of our God, I'm go-ing home at last.
with me, so my soul will have no dread, I'm go-ing home at last.

CHORUS.

I'm go-ing home at last, I'm go-ing home at last; When my
at last, at last;

work on earth is end-ed and my race below is run, I'm going home at last.

"WEEP NOT FOR ME."

Rev. Johnson Oatman, Jr.   (Luke 23 : 28.)   W. F. Fowler.

Andante.

pp

Weep not for me,............... weep not for me, for me.
Weep not for me,   weep not for me.

Sostenuto.

1. Tho' o'er my life-less form you may be bend - ing, For now my song with
2. But think of me as on - ly gone be - fore you; From heav'nly heights I
3. Tho' now with grief your heart is sad and ach - ing, Tho' now with sobs your
4. Tho' now you feel a sense of des - o - la - tion, For those who mourn there
5. Tho' 'tis God's will that earthly ties should sev - er, We'll meet again, where

an - gel notes is blend - ing; I'm safe at home, where joys are nev - er
will be watching o'er you, Just by the gates I will be wait - ing
bo - som may be shak - ing; Mine eyes have seen the gold- en morning
is a con - so - la - tion; In heav'n a - bove will come no sep - a -
part - ing com - eth nev - er; There, hand in hand, we'll live and love for

Chorus.

end - ing, Weep not for me. Dear friends, weep not for me, but still your
for you, Weep not for me.
break - ing, Weep not for me.
ra - tion, Weep not for me.
ev - er, Weep not for me.

Weep not, but still your

sor - row, Dear friends, weep not for me, but com- fort bor - row; In
Weep not,

heav'n a - bove we'll meet a- gain to - mor - row, Weep not for me.

OUR BLEST REDEEMER, ERE HE BREATHED.

HARRIET AUBER.   J. B. DYKES.

1. Our blest Redeem - er, ere he breathed His ten - der, last farewell,
2. He came, sweet influence to im- part, A gracious, will - ing Guest,
3. And ev - 'ry vir - tue we pos- sess, And ev - 'ry vic - t'ry won,
4. Spir - it of pur - i - ty and grace! Our weakness pity - ing see;

A Guide, a Com - fort - er bequeathed, With us to dwell.
While he can find one hum - ble heart Where - in to rest.
And ev - 'ry thought of ho - li - ness Is his a - lone.
Oh, make our hearts thy dwell - ing place, And worth - ier thee!

"OLD GLORY."

F. E. PETTENGELL.

GEO. C. HUGG.

Maestoso.

1. Heirs of our na-tion de-light in Old Glo-ry, Give it your
2. Gath-er the children beneath its pro-tec-tion, Tell them its
3. O-ver each building that fos-ters the stu-dent, Be _its con-
4. O that it ruled in the land of up-rightness, O that its
5. God of all kingdoms, all na-tions, all peo-ples, Let us thy

hom-age, its prow-ess maintain; Flag of our fath-ers, their
sto-ry, its pur-port ex-plain; Teach them with rev-er-ent
struc-tion im-pos-ing or plain; O-ver each earn-est, each
sub-jects all wrongs would dis-dain; O that it knew not of
fa-vor, thy bless-ing re-tain; Help us to fol-low the

cost-ly pos-ses-sion, Purchased with dan-ger, with heart-throb, with pain;
love to behold it, Ev-er to guard it from trai-tors' foul stain;
hon-est as-sem-bly, Where loy-al pre-cept and pur-pose ob-tain;
greed, of op-pression, Par-ti-san meanness, or un-righteous gain;
mar-vel-ous message, Chanted by an-gels o'er Beth-le-hem's plain;

Fling to the heav-ens, from tow-er and top-mast, Let it float
Then shall its stars and its stripes be un-sul-lied, As it floats
O-ver the homesteads, by in-land and sea-side, Let it float
Make it, ye peo-ple, a no-ble in-cen-tive, As it floats
Then shall our ban-ner claim old and new glo-ry, As it floats

CHORUS.

proudly a- bove its domain.
proudly around its domain.
proudly throughout its domain.
proudly around its domain.
proudly a- bove its domain.

Old Glo-ry ! Old Glo- ry ! our nations bright

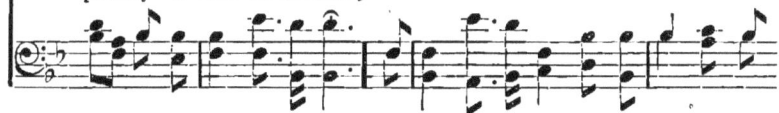

banner, Studded with honors and glowing with fame; Old Glory! Old Glory! our

tro- phy, our treasure, Let the glad cho - ral its prais - es proclaim.

GOD OF NATIONS. L. M.

1 Great God of nations, now to thee
Our hymn of gratitude we raise ;
With humble heart and bending knee
We offer thee our song of praise.

2 Thy name we bless, Almighty God,
For all the kindness thou hast shown
To this fair land the pilgrims trod—
This land we fondly call our own.

3 Here freedom spreads her banner wide,
And casts her soft and hallowed ray ;
Here thou our fathers' steps didst guide
In safety thro' their dangerous way.

4 We praise thee that the gospel's light
Thro' all our land its radiance sheds ;
Dispels the shades of error's night,
And heavenly blessings round us spreads.
—Unknown.

OUR FATHERS' GOD. L. M.

1 To thee, O God, whose guiding hand
Our fathers led across the sea,
And brought them to this barren shore,
Where they might freely worship thee—

2 To thee, O God, whose arm sustained
Their footsteps in this barren land,
Where sickness lurked and death assailed,
And foes beset on every hand—

3 To thee, O God, we lift our eyes ;
To thee our grateful voices raise ;
And, kneeling at thy gracious throne,
Devoutly join in hymns of praise.

4 Our fathers' God, incline thine ear,
And listen to our heartfelt prayer ;
Surround us with thy heavenly grace,
And guard us with thy constant care.
—W. T. Davis.

MY COUNTRY, 'TIS OF THEE.

S. F. Smith. (American Tune.) A. A. DuBois.

VOICES IN UNISON.

1. My coun - try ! 'tis of thee, Sweet land of lib - er - ty.
2. My na - tive coun - try, thee, Land of the no - ble, free,
3. Our fa - thers' God ! to thee, Au - thor of lib - er - ty,

Of thee I sing : Land where my fa - thers died ! Land of the
Thy name I love ; I love thy rocks and rills, Thy woods and
To thee we sing : Long may our land be bright With freedom's

pilgrims' pride ! From ev - 'ry moun - tain side Let free-dom ring !
tem - pled hills : My heart with rap - ture thrills Like that a - bove.
ho - ly light ; Pro - tect us by thy might, Great God, our King !

TRUST GOD. L. M.

1 Now may the God of grace and power
  Attend his people's humble cry ;
Defend them in the needful hour
And send deliverance from on high.

2 In his salvation is our hope ;
  And in the name of Israel's God
Our troops shall lift our banners up,
  Our navies spread their flags abroad.

3 Some trust in horses trained for war,
  And some of chariots make their boasts ;
Our surest expectations are
From thee, the Lord of heavenly hosts.

4 Then, save us, Lord, from slavish fear,
  And let our trust be firm and strong,
Till thy salvation shall appear,
  And hymns of peace conclude our song.
  —Isaac Watts.

GUARD AND GUIDE US. C. M.

1 Lord, while for all mankind we pray,
  Of every clime and coast,
O hear us for our native land—
  The land we love the most.

2 O guard our shores from every foe ;
  With peace our borders bless ;
Our cities with prosperity ;
  Our fields with plenteousness.

3 Unite us in the sacred love
  Of knowledge, truth and thee ;
And let our hills and valleys shout
  The songs of liberty.

4 Lord of the nations, thus to thee
  Our country we commend ;
Be thou her refuge and her trust,
  Her everlasting friend.
  —J. R. Wreford.

GIVE US THE BATTLE.

Ida L. Reed.   W. F. Fowler.

f

1. Give us the battle, Lord Je - ho - vah, Strongly the foes beset us 'round;
2. Give us the battle, lead us on - ward. Help us to triumph o - ver sin;
3. Give us the battle, we are read - y Onward to move at thy com - mand;
4. Give us the battle, Lord Je - ho - vah, Strengthen thy legions for the fight;

Strengthen our hearts for the con - flict, Let thy sustain - ing grace abound.
Self, thro' thy love, may we con - quer, Keep thou our frail hearts pure within.
On thy sure promises re - ly - ing, Firm - ly for thee, dear Lord, we stand.
Strong are the foes that be - set us, Give us thy grace and ho - ly might.

Chorus.
Unison.   Parts.   Unison.   Parts.

Give us the battle, Lord Je- ho- vah, Lead us to vic- to- ry in thy name;

ff

Give us the battle, Lord Je - hovah, Wilt thou thy might and thy pow'r proclaim?

RED, WHITE AND BLUE.

ARR. by FRANK L. ARMSTRONG.

Allegro.

1. O Co- lum - bia, the gem of the o- cean,   The home of the
2. When war wing'd its wide des - o - la- tion,   And threatened the
3. The star - spangled ban- ner bring hither,   O'er Co- lumbia's true

brave and the free,   The shrine of each pa - triot's de - vo- tion,
land to de - form,   The ark then of free-dom's foundation,
sons let it wave ;   May the wreaths they have won nev- er with- er,

A world of - fers hom- age to thee,   Thy mandates make
Co - lum - bia, rode safe thro' the storm: With the garlands of
Nor its stars cease to shine on the brave. May the ser - vice u-

he - roes as - sem- ble,   When Lib - er - ty's form stands in view ;
vic- t'ry around her, When so proud- ly she bore her brave crew,
ni - ted ne'er sev - er,   But hold to their col - ors so true ;

Thy ban-ners make tyr - an - ny trem - ble, When
With her flag proud - ly float - ing be - fore her, The
The arm - y and na - vy for - ev - er, Three

borne by the red, white and blue, When borne by the red, white and blue,
boast of the red, white and blue, The boast of the red, white and blue,
cheers for the red, white and blue, Three cheers for the red, white and blue,

When borne by the red, white and blue, Thy banners make tyr - an - ny
The boast of the red, white and blue, With her flag floating proudly be-
Three cheers for the red, white and blue, The arm - y and na - vy for-

trem - ble, When borne by the red, white and blue.
fore her, The boast of the red, white and blue.
ev - er, Three cheers for the red, white and blue.

FRANCIS SCOTT KEY. 1814.

VOICES IN UNISON.

1. Oh, say, can you see, by the dawn's ear - ly light,
2. On the shore dim - ly seen thro' the mists of the deep,
3. And where is that band who so vaunt - ing - ly swore,
4. Oh, thus be it ev - er when free—men shall stand

What so proud - ly we hailed at the twilight's last gleaming,
Where the foe's haughty host in dread si - lence re - pos - es,
That the hav - oc of war and the bat - tle's con - fu - sion,
Between their lov - ed home and wild war's des - o - la - tion;

Whose broad stripes and bright stars, thro' the per - i - lous fight,
What is that which the breeze, o'er the tow - er - ing steep,
A home and a coun - try should leave us no more?
Blest with vic - t'ry and peace, may the heav'n - res - cued land

O'er the ram - parts we watched, were so gal - lant - ly streaming?
As it fit - ful - ly blows, half con - ceals, half dis - clos - es?
Their blood has washed out their foul foot - steps' pol - lu - tion.
Praise the Pow'r that hath made and preserv'd us a na - tion!

And the rock - ets' red glare, the bombs burst - ing in air,
Now it catch - es the gleam of the morning's first beam,
No ref - uge could save the hire - ling and slave
Then con - quer we must, when our cause it is just,

Gave proof thro' the night that our flag was still there.
In full glo - ry re - flect - ed, now shines on the stream:
From the ter - ror of flight or the gloom of the grave:
And this be our mot - to: "In God is our trust!"

CHORUS.

Oh, say, does that star - spangled ban - ner yet wave
'Tis the star - spangled ban - ner: oh, long may it wave
And the star - spangled ban - ner in tri - umph doth wave
And the star - spangled ban - ner in tri - umph shall wave

O'er the land of the free and the home of the brave.

OUR NATION.

REV. JOHNSON OATMAN, JR.   J. HOWARD ENTWISLE.

1. A bright con-stel-la-tion il-lumines the sky, Where ev-er our
2. The streams that are flow-ing out toward the great sea, The winds that are
3. No mon-arch his scep-tre waves o-ver the land, Here king-doms would
4. O ref-uge for Pilgrims for all earth's oppressed, Thy bea-con is
5. May dis-tant O-ri-on, may Sa-turn and Mars, For-ev-er look

ban-ner floats proud-ly on high, The en-sign of free-dom, its
blow-ing all breathe lib-er-ty, The ea-gle now soar-ing in
per-ish here thrones can-not stand, Here *home* is the king-dom by
shin-ing a-cross the dark crest, A light to the na-tion's may
down on our ban-ner of stars, Our sons and our daughters this

folds rise and fall, O'er earth's rich-est coun-try and great-est of all.
heav-en's blue dome, Looks down on a coun-try which free men call home.
ty-rants ne'er trod, This land knows no ru-ler save Al-might-y God.
it ev-er be, The fair-est and brightest, the Queen of the sea.
dear land de-fend, Un-til time and na-tions have come to an end.

CHORUS.

I love thee, I love thee, O land of the free, Thy hills and thy val - leys are pre - cious to me; I love thee, I love thee, thou

land of the West, Of all the great na - tions, the last and the best.

ROCK OF AGES.

A. M. TOPLADY.

THOS. HASTINGS.

FINE.

1. Rock of A - ges, cleft for me, Let me hide my-self in Thee;
D. C.—Be of sin the dou - ble cure—Cleanse me from its guilt and power.

D. C.

Let the wa - ter and the blood, From Thy riv - en side which flow'd.

2. Not the labor of my hands
Can fulfill the law's demands;
Could my zeal no respite know,
Could my tears forever flow,
All for sin could not atone—
Thou must save and Thou alone.

3. Nothing in my hand I bring;
Simply to Thy cross I cling;
Naked, come to Thee for dress;

Helpless, look to Thee for grace;
Foul, I to the fountain fly;
Wash me, Saviour, or I die.

4. While I draw this fleeting breath,
When my heart-strings break in death,
When I soar to worlds unknown,
See Thee on Thy judgment throne,
Rock of Ages cleft for me,
Let me hide myself in Thee.

210

ON TO VICTORY.

J. H. E.   J. Howard Entwisle.

1. Hark! hark, the trumpet sound - ing, Rise at the break of day,
2. March-ing like val - iant sol - diers, Stead - y our steps and true,
3. Then shall the path be bright - er, No more by care op - press'd,

On to the front where sin is a-bound-ing, Forward the call o - bey,
Faith in our Lead- er, no thought of dan-ger, Fear and alarm, a - dieu,
Firm in our pur - pose, true in our motives, Hop-ing for what is best,

Put on the gos - pel ar - mor, Go forth in faith to con - quer,
On, though the world op-press thee, On, though the foe dis - tress thee,
Trust-ing the King of glo - ry, Tell - ing the old, old sto - ry,

Hear, hear the Captain's words in - spir - ing, on, soldiers, on to the fray.
Stead-fast and firm, keep moving on till fair Canaan's land stands in view.
Wait-ing the Master's call to en - ter in - to the Ha - ven of Rest.

CHORUS.

Forward, then, with banners waving high, Forward, as we shout the battle cry,

Onward in the con-flict, hop-ing, trust-ing, on to vic-to-ry!

UXBRIDGE.

HARRIET AUBER. LOWELL MASON.

1. Ere mountains reared their forms sublime, Or heav'n and earth in or - der stood;
2. A thousand a-ges in their flight, With thee are as a fleet-ing day;
3. But our brief life's a shadowy dream, A passing tho't, that soon is o'er,
4. To us, O Lord, the wisdom give Each passing mo-ment so to spend

Be-fore the birth of an - cient time, From ev-er-last-ing, Thou art God.
Past, present, future to Thy sight At once their various scenes dis-play.
That fades with morning's earliest beam, And fills the musing mind no more.
That we at length with Thee may live, Where life and bliss shall never end.

I'VE ENTERED THE HARBOR OF PEACE.

W. E. M.

WM. EDIE MARKS.

1. I'm tran-quil-ly rest-ing, No storms are op-press-ing, I've
2. The strug-gles were ma-ny, My trou-bles were plen-ty, And
3. I'm safe in its shel-ter From all storm-y weath-er; I've

en-tered the har-bor of peace; I've passed from the o-cean Of
they always seem to in - crease; But now they are o-ver, I've
en-tered the har-bor of peace; And here 'neath its cov-er I'll

sin and com-mo-tion, I've en-tered the har-bor of peace.
en-tered the har-bor, The beau-ti-ful har-bor of peace.
an-chor for-ev-er; I've en-tered the har-bor of peace.

CHORUS.

I'm tran - - quil-ly rest - ing, I've
I'm tran-quil-ly rest-ing, I'm tran-quil-ly rest-ing,

en- tered the har- bor of peace; This ref - uge so precious was

giv - en by Je - sus; I've en - tered the har- bor of peace.

GET THEE BEHIND ME, SATAN.

WILLIAM HUGHES.   V. PAUL JONES.

1. Get thee behind me, Sa - tan, Let thy pre-vail- ings cease;
2. Get thee behind me, Sa - tan, Thou canst not bid me stay;
3. Get thee behind me, Sa - tan, I bid farewell to thee;

Thy path I have a - ban-doned, From sin I've found re - lease.
I'm trav'ling on to glo - ry A - long the King's highway.
I'm go - ing on with Je - sus To God and vic - to - ry.

SPEED THE LIGHT.

E. A. H.

Rev. Elisha A. Hoffman.

1. To the mill-ions liv-ing o'er the deep, deep sea   Speed the
2. There in an-guish mill-ions for the gos-pel wait,   Speed the
3. Je-sus bids us bear to them the gos-pel news,   Speed the
4. We will go, and in our bless-ed Mas-ter's name   Speed the

light,......... speed the light ;   To their cry of pit-y dare we
light,......... speed the light ;   Go and seek their res-cue ere it
light,......... speed the light ;   Can the souls be ransomed his re-
light,... ...... speed the light ;   We will his sal-va-tion and his

Speed the light,   speed the light ;

heed-less be? Speed the light,..........   O speed the light !
is too late, Speed the light,..........   O speed the light !
quest re-fuse, Speed the light,..........   O speed the light !
love proclaim, Speed the light,..........   O speed the light !

Speed the light,   O speed the light !

Chorus.

Speed the light,.......... the bless-ed gos-pel light, To the lands........

Speed the light,   To the

which are in gloom and night; Souls are wait - ing, and the
lands   Souls are waiting,

fields are white; Speed the light,........ O speed the light!
Speed the light,   O speed the light!

SEYMOUR. 7.

JOHN NEWTON.   CARL MARIA VON WEBER.

1. Come, my soul, thy suit pre-pare, Je-sus loves to answer prayer;
2. Lord, I come to thee for rest; Take pos-ses-sion of my breast;
3. While I am a pil-grim here, Let thy love my spir-it cheer;
4. Show me what I have to do; Ev-'ry hour my strength re-new;

He him-self in-vites thee near, Bids thee ask him, waits to hear.
There thy blood-bought right main-tain, And with-out a ri-val reign.
As my guide, my guard, my friend, Lead me to my journey's end.
Let me live a life of faith, Let me die thy people's death.

THE LAND OF BEULAH.—Key G.

I am dwelling on the mountain,
   Where the golden sunlight gleams,
O'er a land whose wondrous beauty
   Far exceeds my fondest dreams ;
Where the air is pure, ethereal,
   Laden with the breath of flowers,
They are blooming by the fountain,
   'Neath the amaranthine bowers.

CHO.—Is not this the land of Beulah,
     Blessed, blessed land of light,
   Where the flowers bloom forever,
     And the sun is always bright?

2 I can see far down the mountain,
   Where I wandered weary years,
Often hindered in my journey
   By the ghosts of doubts and fears,
Broken vows and disappointments
   Thickly sprinkled all the way,
But the Spirit led, unerring,
   To the land I hold to-day.

3 I am drinking at the fountain,
   Where I would abide ;
For I've tasted life's pure river,
   And my soul is satisfied ;
There's no thirsting for life's pleasures,
   Nor adorning, rich and gay,
For I've found a richer treasure,
   One that fadeth not away.

HAPPY DAY.—Key G.

O happy day that fixed my choice
   On thee, my Saviour and my God !
Well may this glowing heart rejoice,
   And tell its raptures all abroad.

2 O happy bond, that seals my vows
   To him who merits all my love !
Let cheerful anthems fill his house,
   While to that sacred shrine I move.

3 'Tis done, the great transaction's
    done ;
   I am my Lord's, and he is mine ;
He drew me, and I followed on,
   Charmed to confess the voice divine.

4 Now rest, my long-divided heart ;
   Fixed on this blissful centre, rest ;
Nor ever from thy Lord depart,
   With him of every good possessed.

5 High Heaven, that heard the solemn
    vow,
   That vow renewed shall daily hear
Till in life's latest hour I bow,
   And bless in death a bond so dear.

MISSIONARY HYMN.—Key F.

From Greenland's icy mountains,
   From India's coral strand ;
Where Afric's sunny fountains
   Roll down their golden sand ;
From many an ancient river,
   From many a palmy plain,
They call us to deliver
   Their land from error's chain.

2 Shall we, whose souls are lighted
   With wisdom from on high,
Shall we, to men benighted,
   The lamp of life deny?
Salvation ! oh, salvation !
   The joyful sound proclaim,
Till earth's remotest nation
   Has learned Messiah's name.

3 Waft, waft, ye winds, His story ;
   And you, ye waters, roll,
Till, like a sea of glory,
   It spreads from pole to pole ;
Till o'er our ransomed nature,
   The Lamb for sinners slain,
Redeemer, King, Creator,
   In bliss returns to reign.

BRINGING IN THE SHEAVES.—Key C.

Sowing in the morning, sowing seeds of
   kindness,
   Sowing in the noon-tide, and the dewy
    eves ;
Waiting for the harvest, and the time of
   reaping,
   We shall come rejoicing, bringing in
    the sheaves.

CHO.—||: Bringing in the sheaves, :||
   We shall come rejoicing, bringing in
    the sheaves.

2 Sowing in the sunshine, sowing in the
   shadows,
   Fearing neither clouds, nor winter's
    chilling breeze ;
By and by the harvest, and the labor
   ended,
   We shall come rejoicing, bringing in
    the sheaves.

3 Go, then, ever weeping, sowing for
   the Master,
   Though the loss sustained our spirit
    often grieves ;
When our weeping's over He will bid
   us welcome,
   We shall come rejoicing, bringing in
    the sheaves.

ON JESUS.

I lay my sins on Jesus,
　The spotless Lamb of God ;
He bears them all, and frees us
　From the accursed load :
I bring my guilt to Jesus,
　To wash my crimson stains
White in his blood most precious,
　Till not a stain remains.

2 I lay my wants on Jesus ;
　All fullness dwells in him ;
He healeth my diseases,
　He doth my soul redeem :
I lay my griefs on Jesus,
　My burdens and my cares ;
He from them all releases,
　He all my sorrows shares.

3 I rest my soul on Jesus,
　This weary soul of mine ;
His right hand me embraces,
　I on his breast recline ;
I love the name of Jesus,
　Immanuel, Christ, the Lord ;
Like fragrance on the breezes,
　His name abroad is poured.

4 I long to be like Jesus,
　Meek, loving, lowly, mild ;
I long to be like Jesus,
　The Father's holy child :
I long to be with Jesus,
　Amid the heavenly throng,
To sing with saints his praises,
　And learn the angels' song.

BETHANY.—Key G.

Nearer, my God, to thee !
　Nearer to thee,
E'en though it be a cross
　That raiseth me ;
Still all my song shall be,
"Nearer, my God, to thee,
　Nearer to thee !"

2 Though like a wanderer,
　The sun gone down,
Darkness be over me,
　My rest a stone,
Yet in my dreams I'd be
Nearer, my God, to thee,
　Nearer to thee !

3 There let my way appear,
　Steps unto heaven ;
All that thou sendest me,
　In mercy given ;
Angels to beckon me
Nearer, my God, to thee,
　Nearer to thee !
　　　　　　　—Mrs. S. F. Adams.

HOLY GHOST, WITH LIGHT DI-VINE.—Martin, Key F.

Holy Ghost, with light divine,
Shine upon this heart of mine ;
Chase the shades of night away,
Turn my darkness into day.

2 Holy Ghost, with power divine,
Cleanse this guilty heart of mine ;
Long hath sin, without control,
Held dominion o'er my soul.

3 Holy Ghost, with joy divine,
Cheer this saddened heart of mine ;
Bid my many woes depart,
Heal my wounded, bleeding heart.

4 Holy Spirit, all divine,
Dwell within this heart of mine ;
Cast down ev'ry idol-throne,
Reign supreme—and reign alone.
　　　　　　　—A. Reed.

AT THE CROSS.

Alas ! and did my Saviour bleed,
　And did my sovereign die ?
Would he devote that sacred head
　For such a worm as I ?

CHO.—At the cross, at the cross,
　Where I first saw the light,
And the burden of my heart rolled away,
　It was there by faith
　I received my sight,
And now I am happy all the day.

2 Was it for crimes that I had done,
　He groaned upon the tree ?
Amazing pity, grace unknown,
　And love beyond degree !

3 But drops of grief can ne'er repay
　The debt of love I owe ;
Here, Lord, I give myself away
　'Tis all that I can do !
　　　　　　　—I. Watts.

WORK.—Key F.

Work, for the night is coming,
　Work through the morning hours ;
Work, while the dew is sparkling,
　Work 'mid springing flowers ;
Work, when the day grows brighter,
　Work, in the glowing sun ;
Work, for the night is coming,
　When man's work is done.

2 Work, for the night is coming,
　Work through the sunny noon ;
Fill brightest hours with labor,
　Rest comes sure and soon.
Give every flying minute
　Something to keep in store ;
Work, for the night is coming,
　When man works no more.
　　　　　　　—Annie Walker.

COME TO JESUS.—Key G.

Come to Jesus, come to Jesus !
2 He will save you!
3 Oh, believe him!
4 He is able.
5 He is willing.
6 He'll receive you
7 Call upon him !
8 He will hear you.
9 Look unto him !
10 He'll forgive you.
11 Flee to Jesus !
12 He will cleanse you.
13 He will clothe you.
14 Jesus loves you.
15 Don't reject him !
16 Only trust him !
17 Hallelujah, Amen !

MATCHLESS WORTH.

O could I speak the matchless worth,
O could I sound the glories forth,
   Which in my Saviour shine,
I'd soar and touch the heavenly strings
And vie with Gabriel while he sings
   In notes almost divine.

2 I'd sing the precious blood he spilt,
My ransom from the dreadful guilt
   Of sin, and wrath divine ;
I'd sing his glorious righteousness,
In which all-perfect, heavenly dress
   My soul shall ever shine.

HOLY SPIRIT.—Key G.

Holy Spirit, faithful guide,
Ever near the Christian's side,
Gently lead us by the hand,
Pilgrims in a desert land ;
Weary souls for e'er rejoice,
While they hear that sweetest voice
Whispering softly, "Wanderer, come !
Follow me, I'll guide thee home."

2 Ever-present, truest friend,
Ever near thine aid to lend,
Leave us not to doubt and fear,
Groping on in darkness drear ;
When the storms are raging sore,
Hearts grow faint, and hopes give o'er,
Whisper softly, "Wanderer, come !
Follow me, I'll guide thee home."
          —M. M. Wells.

LORD'S PROTECTION.—Hebron,
L. M., Key B♭.

Thus far the Lord hath led me on,
   Thus far his power prolonged my days;
And every evening shall make known
   Some fresh memorial of his grace.

2 Much of my time has run to waste,
   And I, perhaps, am near my home ;
But he forgives my follies past,
   He gives me strength for days to come.

3 I lay my body down to sleep ;
   Peace is the pillow for my head,
While well appointed angels keep
   Their watchful stations round my bed.

4 Thus, when the night of death shall come,
   My flesh shall rest beneath the ground,
And wait thy voice to break my tomb,
   With sweet salvation in the sound.
          —Isaac Watts.

SWEET HOUR.—Key D.

Sweet hour of prayer, sweet hour of prayer,
That calls me from a world of care,
And bids me, at my Father's throne,
Make all my wants and wishes known !
In seasons of distress and grief,
My soul has often found relief,
And oft escaped the tempter's snare,
By thy return, sweet hour of prayer.

2 Sweet hour of prayer, sweet hour of prayer,
May I thy consolation share,
Till, from Mount Pisgah's lofty height,
I view my home, and take my flight !
This robe of flesh I'll drop, and rise
To seize the everlasting prize ;
And shout, while passing through the air,
Farewell, farewell, sweet hour of prayer !
          —W. W. Walford.

THE CHILD OF A KING.—Key F.

My Father is rich
   In houses and lands,
He holdeth the wealth
   Of the world in his hands !
Of rubies and diamonds,
   Of silver and gold
His coffers are full,
   He has riches untold !

Cho.—I'm the child of a King !
   The child of a King !
With Jesus, my Saviour,
   I'm the child of a King.

2 A tent or a cottage,
   Why should I care?
They're building a palace
   For me over there.
Though exiled from home,
   Yet still I may sing :
"All glory to God,
   I'm the child of a King."
          —H. E. Buell.

WEBB.—Key B♭.

Stand up, stand up for Jesus,
   Ye soldiers of the cross ;
Lift high his royal banner,
   It must not suffer loss :
From victory unto victory
   His army shall he lead,
Till every foe is vanquished
   And Christ is Lord indeed.

2 Stand up, stand up for Jesus,
   The trumpet call obey ;
Forth to the mighty conflict,
   In this his glorious day :
"Ye that are men, now serve him,"
   Against unnumbered foes ;
Your courage rise with danger,
   And strength to strength oppose.
          —Geo. Duffield, Jr.

SILVER ST.—Key C.

Grace ! 'tis a charming sound,
    Harmonious to the ear ;
Heaven with the echo shall resound,
    And all the earth shall hear.

2 Grace first contrived a way
    To save rebellious man ;
And all the steps that grace display,
    Which drew the wondrous plan.

3 Grace taught my roving feet
    To tread the heavenly road ;
And new supplies each hour I meet,
    While pressing on to God.

4 Grace all the work shall crown
    Through everlasting days ;
It lays in heaven the topmost stone,
    And well deserves our praise.
              —Philip Doddridge.

COME, HOLY SPIRIT.

Come, Holy Spirit, calm my mind,
    And fit me to approach my God ;
Remove each vain, each worldly thought,
    And lead me to the blest abode.

2 Hast thou imparted to my soul
    A living spark of holy fire?
Oh ! kindle now the sacred flame,
    Make me to burn with pure desire.

3 A brighter faith and hope impart,
    And let me now my Saviour see ;
Oh ! soothe and cheer my burdened heart
    And bid my spirit rest in thee.

HE LEADETH ME.—Key D.

He leadeth me ! O blessed thought !
O words with heavenly comfort fraught !
Whate'er I do, where'er I be,
Still 'tis God's hand that leadeth me.

CHO.—He leadeth me, he leadeth me,
    By his own hand he leadeth me ;
    His faithful follower I would be,
    For by his hand he leadeth me.

CLEANSING FOUNTAIN.—Key C.

There is a fountain filled with blood
    Drawn from Immanuel's veins ;
And sinners, plunged beneath that flood,
    Lose all their guilty stains.

2 The dying thief rejoiced to see
    That fountain in his day ;
And there may I, though vile as he,
    Wash all my sins away.

3 Thou dying Lamb ! thy precious blood
    Shall never lose its power
Till all the ransomed Church of God
    Are saved, to sin no more.
       . —Wm. Cowper.

THE SOLID ROCK.—Key G.

My hope is built on nothing less
Than Jesus' blood and righteousness ;
I dare not trust the sweetest frame,
But wholly lean on Jesus' name :
On Christ, the solid rock, I stand ;
‖: All other ground is sinking sand. :‖

2 When darkness seems to veil his face,
I rest on his unchanging grace ;
In every high and stormy gale,
My anchor holds within the veil :
On Christ, the solid rock, I stand ;
‖: All other ground is sinking sand. :‖
              —Edward Mote.

ONLY TRUST HIM.—Key G.

Come, every soul by sin oppressed,
There's mercy with the Lord,
And he will surely give you rest,
By trusting in his word.

CHO.—Only trust him, only trust him
    Only trust him now ;
He will save you, he will save you,
    He will save you now.

2 For Jesus shed his precious blood
    Rich blessings to bestow ;
Plunge now into the crimson flood
    That washes white as snow.

DUNDEE.—Key Eb.

Come, Holy Spirit, heav'nly Dove,
    With all thy quick'ning powers ;
Kindle a flame of sacred love
    In these cold hearts of ours.

2 Father, and shall we ever live
    At this poor dying rate—
Our love so faint, so cold to thee,
    And thine to us so great ?

3 Come, Holy Spirit, heav'nly Dove,
    With all thy quick'ning powers ;
Come, shed abroad a Saviour's love,
    And that shall kindle ours.
              —Isaac Watts.

DENNIS.—Key F.

Blest be the tie that binds
    Our hearts in Christian love ;
The fellowship of kindred minds
    Is like to that above.

2 Before our Father's throne,
    We pour our ardent prayers ;
Our fears, our hopes, our aims are one,
    Our comforts, and our cares.

3 We share our mutual woes,
    Our mutual burdens bear ;
And often for each other flows
    The sympathizing tear.

4 When we asunder part,
    It gives us inward pain ;
But we shall still be joined in heart,
    And hope to meet again.
              —John Fawcett.

LENNOX.—Key B♭.

Arise, my soul, arise,
 Shake off thy guilty fears;
The bleeding Sacrifice
 In my behalf appears:
Before the throne my Surety stands
My name is written on his hands.

2 He ever lives above,
 For me to intercede;
His all-redeeming love,
 His precious blood to plead:
His blood atoned for all our race,
And sprinkles now the throne of grace.

3 Five bleeding wounds he bears,
 Received on Calvary;
They pour effectual prayers,
 They strongly plead for me:
"Forgive him, O forgive," they cry,
"Nor let that ransomed sinner die."

4 My God is reconciled;
 His pardoning voice I hear;
He owns me for his child;
 I can no longer fear:
With confidence I now draw nigh,
And, "Father, Abba, Father," cry.
 —Charles Wesley.

RATHBUN.—Key C.

In the cross of Christ I glory,
Tow'ring o'er the wrecks of time;
All the light of sacred story
Gathers round its head sublime.

2 When the woes of life o'ertake me,
 Hopes deceive and fears annoy,
Never shall the cross forsake me—
 Lo! it glows with peace and joy.

3 Bane and blessing, pain and pleasure,
 By the cross are sanctified;
Peace is there, that knows no measure,
 Joys that through all time abide.
 —John Bowring.

EVAN.—Key A♭.

Forever here my rest shall be,
Close to thy bleeding side;
This all my hope and all my plea—
For me the Saviour died.

Cho.—‖: Blessed be the name,:‖
 Blessed be the name of the Lord;
 ‖: Blessed be the name,:‖
 Blessed be the name of the Lord.

2 My dying Saviour and my God,
 Fountain for guilt and sin,
Sprinkle me ever with thy blood,
 And cleanse and keep me clean.

3 Wash me, and make me thus thine own:
 Wash me, and mine thou art;
Wash me, but not my feet alone,—
 My hands, my head, my heart.

4 Th' atonement of thy blood apply,
 Till faith to sight improve;
Till hope in full fruition die,
 And all my soul be love.
 —Charles Wesley.

**I AM COMING TO THE CROSS.—
Key G.**

I am coming to the cross,
 I am poor and weak and blind;
I am counting all but dross,
 I shall full salvation find.

Cho.—I am trusting, Lord, in thee;
 Blessed Lamb of Calvary;
 Humbly at the cross I bow;
 Jesus saves me—saves me now.

2 Long my heart has sighed for thee,
 Long has evil dwelt within;
Jesus sweetly speaks to me;
 "I will cleanse you from all sin."

3 Here I give my all to thee,
 Friends, and time, and earthly store,
Soul and body thine to be—
 Wholly thine for evermore.

4 In the promises I trust,
 In the cleansing blood confide;
I am prostrate in the dust,
 I with Christ am crucified.

5 Jesus comes, he fills my soul,
 Perfected in him I am,
I am every whit made whole,
 Glory, glory to the Lamb!—
 —W. McDonald.

MARTYN.—Key F.

Jesus, Lover of my soul,
 Let me to thy bosom fly,
While the nearer waters roll,
 While the tempest still is high!
Hide me, O my Saviour, hide,
 Till the storm of life is past;
Safe into the haven guide,
 O receive my soul at last!

2 Other refuge have I none;
 Hangs my helpless soul on thee:
Leave, O leave me not alone,
 Still support and comfort me:
All my trust on thee is stayed,
 All my help from thee I bring;
Cover my defenceless head
 With the shadow of thy wing!

3 Thou, O Christ, art all I want;
 More than all in thee I find;
Raise the fallen, cheer the faint,
 Heal the sick, and lead the blind.
Just and holy is thy name,
 I am all unrighteousness:
Vile and full of sin I am,
 Thou art full of truth and grace.
 —Charles Wesley.

INDEX OF TITLES.

221

222

INDEX OF TITLES.

INDEX OF FIRST LINES.

www.ingramcontent.com/pod-product-compliance
Lightning Source LLC
Chambersburg PA
CBHW030321270326
41926CB00010B/1454